Macmillan
Mathematics
Pupil's book

6A

Paul Broadbent

MACMILLAN

Contents

BLOCK A   Understanding numbers

BLOCK B   Numerical operations

BLOCK C Geometry

Unit 1　Integers and decimals

Integers

> All whole numbers are called integers.
> Integers can be positive or negative.
> Zero is an integer.
>
> Remember…
> When you move left on a number line, numbers get smaller, when you move right on a number line, numbers get larger.
>
> > ≤ means 'less than or equal to'
> > ≥ means 'greater than or equal to'

1 To which number does each arrow point?

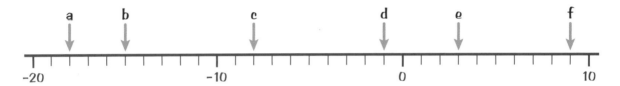

2 Look at the number line above. Write the difference between these numbers.

a) a and c　　　　**b)** d and e　　　　**c)** b and f　　　　**d)** e and a

3 Which integers could go in the boxes?

a) $-4 < \boxed{} < 0$　　**b)** $-11 < \boxed{} < -8$　　**c)** $-3 < \boxed{} < 2$　　**d)** $-21 < \boxed{} < -17$

e) $-9 > \boxed{} > -12$　　**f)** $-1 > \boxed{} > -6$　　**g)** $-5 > \boxed{} > -9$　　**h)** $-19 > \boxed{} > -23$

4 Which integers could go in the boxes?

a) $-7 \leq \boxed{} \leq -2$　　**b)** $-1 \leq \boxed{} \leq 4$　　**c)** $-14 \leq \boxed{} \leq -8$　　**d)** $-6 \leq \boxed{} \leq -1$

e) $0 \geq \boxed{} \geq -5$　　**f)** $-2 \geq \boxed{} \geq -4$　　**g)** $3 \geq \boxed{} \geq -1$　　**h)** $-15 \geq \boxed{} \geq -19$

5 What is the difference in temperature between these pairs of thermometers?

a)
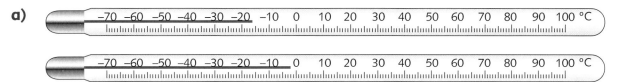

b)
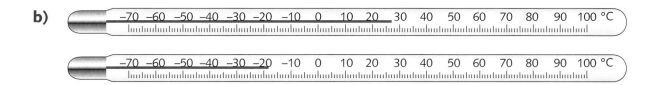

c)
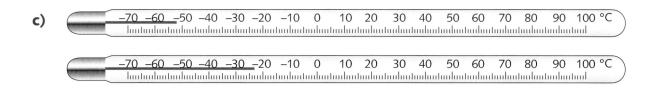

d)
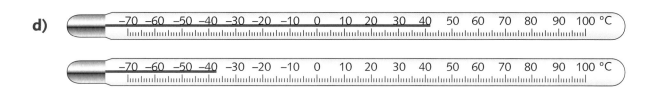

6 Write these temperatures in order, starting with the lowest.

| 38° | | −7° | | −14° | | 0° | | 27° | | −24° |

Try this

Jack was trying to throw a coin exactly 2 metres. He recorded each attempt in centimetres above or below his target.

Attempt	1st	2nd	3rd	4th	5th	6th	7th	8th
Distance from target (cm)	+3	+5	−3	−7	−1	0	+1	−2

a) What was his longest throw in centimetres?
b) What was his shortest throw in centimetres?
c) On which attempt did he hit the target?
d) On which attempt did he throw 197 cm?
e) How would he have recorded a throw of 192 cm?

Rounding and approximation

When working with large numbers, rounding makes them easier to work with.

Remember…
Rounding means changing a number to the nearest 10, 100, 1000, 10 000 or 100 000.

Example

Number	nearest 10	nearest 100	nearest 1000	nearest 10 000
48 193 065	48 193 070	48 193 100	48 193 000	48 190 000

1 Copy and complete this table.

	a) Round to the nearest 100	b) Round to the nearest 1000	c) Round to the nearest 10 000
7 892 388 →			
68 372 105 →			
38 893 465 →			
149 035 476 →			
7 498 024 573 →			
1 093 773 284 →			
1 936 243 225 →			
7 846 374 522 →			

2 Write the smallest and largest numbers that will give the following.

a) 8 460 000 when rounded to the nearest ten thousand.

b) 74 110 000 when rounded to the nearest ten thousand

c) 397 500 000 when rounded to the nearest hundred thousand

d) 649 900 000 when rounded to the nearest hundred thousand

3 Round these numbers.
Decide on the type of rounding to use so that the number you get has just one digit followed by zeros.

a) 44 618   b) 256 700   c) 12 054 000   d) 164 000

e) 11 162   f) 5 602 721   g) 3 532 000   h) 212 500 000

4 Round these distances of the planets from the Sun to the nearest ten thousand, hundred thousand or million.
Decide which one to round to so that the information is still sensible and useful.

Planet	Distance from Sun (km)
Mercury	57 918 438
Venus	108 238 629
Earth	149 621 403
Mars	227 918 304
Jupiter	778 324 941
Saturn	1 427 030 429
Uranus	2 871 302 704
Neptune	4 497 104 396

Try this

a) How many numbers give 7 000 000 when they are rounded to the nearest thousand?

b) How many numbers give 7 000 000 when they are rounded to the nearest ten thousand?

c) How many numbers give 7 000 000 when they are rounded to the nearest hundred thousand?

d) How many numbers give 7 000 000 when they are rounded to the nearest million?

e) Do you get the same results if you choose a different rounded value? Try it for 12 000 000.

f) Can you make any predictions using these results?

Large numbers

Mathematicians often use abbreviations called **index form** to write large numbers in a shorter way. They use powers of 10 to show the number of zeros.

$$10 \times 10 = 10^2 \qquad\qquad 10 \times 10 \times 10 = 10^3 \qquad\qquad 10 \times 10 \times 10 \times 10 = 10^4$$
$$100 = 10^2 \qquad\qquad\qquad 1000 = 10^3 \qquad\qquad\qquad\qquad 10\,000 = 10^4$$

This is how large numbers are written:

$$8400 = 84 \times 10^2 \qquad\qquad 129\,000 = 129 \times 10^3 \qquad\qquad 650\,000 = 65 \times 10^4$$

Did you know?

One billion means one thousand million.
$1\,000\,000\,000 = 10^9$

An American invented the name googol for the number 10^{100}.

1 Write these numbers in full.

a) 67×10^2 b) 5×10^4 c) 85×10^3

d) 23×10^4 e) 38×10^5 f) 162×10^3

g) 15×10^6 h) 32×10^4 i) 12×10^5

j) 11×10^3 k) 294×10^4 l) 2×10^8

2 Write these in index form.

a) 26 000   b) 30 000   c) 294 000

d) 1 800 000   e) 61 000 000   f) 70 000 000

g) 3 810 000   h) 292 000 000   i) 270 000 000

j) 300 000 000   k) 22 000 000   l) 4 830 000 000

3 Copy these sentences, replacing the numbers using index form.

a) The Milky Way is about 100 000 light years across.

b) Astronomers think that there are approximately 200 000 000 000 000 000 000 000 stars.

c) Some stars have a diameter of more than 150 000 000 kilometres.

d) The Sun is approximately 149 000 000 kilometres from Earth.

e) The temperature in the middle of the Sun is approximately 15 000 000°C.

Try this

a) Multiply these two numbers together.

$$10^3 \times 10^4$$

Convert them to full numbers first, then multiply them.

b) Convert the answer into index form.

Do you notice a connection between the answer and the original numbers?

c) Multiply these two numbers together.

$$(2 \times 10^5) \times (4 \times 10^3)$$

Convert them to full numbers first, then multiply them.

d) Convert the answer into index form.

Do you notice a connection between the answer and the original numbers?

Investigate this with some of your own index form multiplications.

Decimal numbers

The decimal point separates whole numbers from decimal fractions.

tens	ones		tenths	hundredths	thousandths	ten thousandths
3	8	.	4	1	5	2
(30)	(8)		$(\frac{4}{10})$	$(\frac{1}{100})$	$(\frac{5}{1000})$	$(\frac{2}{10\,000})$

38.4152 is read as **thirty-eight point four one five two**.

The value of the digit 2 is 2 ten-thousandths or $\frac{2}{10\,000}$, which is a very small fraction!

Decimals are usually rounded to the nearest whole number or nearest tenth.

Rounding to the nearest whole number	**Rounding to the nearest tenth**
• Look at the tenths digit.	• Look at the hundredths digit.
• If it is 5 or more, round up to the next whole number.	• If it is 5 or more, round up to the next tenth.
• If it is less than 5, the units digit stays the same.	• If it is less than 5, the tenth digit stays the same.
18.6209 rounds up to 19	18.5627 rounds up to 18.6
3.3948 rounds down to 3	11.9139 rounds down to 11.9

1 Write the decimal number each arrow points to.

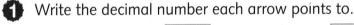

a)

b)

c)

d)

2 Read the decimal numbers from question 1 and write each one in words.

3 Write each set in order, starting with the smallest.

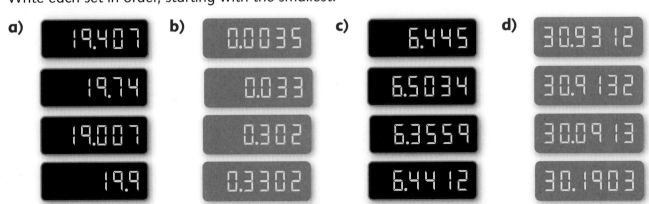

a)
19.407
19.74
19.007
19.9

b)
0.0035
0.033
0.302
0.3302

c)
6.445
6.5034
6.3559
6.4412

d)
30.9312
30.9132
30.0913
30.1903

4 Round each amount to the nearest whole number.

a) 61.39 cm   →   b) 8.085 *l*   →

c) $315.45   →   d) 35.285 g   →

e) 19.62 km   →   f) 18.096 kg   →

5 Round each amount to the nearest tenth.

a) $36.45   →   b) 8.214 litres   →

c) 37.492 m   →   d) 26.743 kg   →

e) 134.264 km   →   f) $37.62   →

6 These are the lengths and weights of some of the smallest mammals in the world.

Mammal	Length (m)	Weight (kg)
African pygmy mouse	0.062	0.0081
Asiatic shrew	0.074	0.0054
Birch mouse	0.073	0.0109
Desert shrew	0.058	0.0038
Pygmy shrew	0.039	0.0025
White-toothed shrew	0.081	0.0113

a) Write the mammals in order of length, starting with the shortest.

b) Write the mammals in order of weight, starting with the lightest.

c) Round each length to the nearest millimetre.

d) Round each weight to the nearest gram.

Try this

a) What number does 3.8025 have to be multiplied by to get 380.25?

b) What number does 518.22 have to be divided by to get 51.822?

c) A number is multiplied by 1000 to give 2.1. What is the number?

d) What number divided by 100 gives 3.0418?

e) A number is divided by 1000 to give 3.610 25. What is the number?

f) A number is multiplied by 1000 to give 29.03. What is the number?

Adding and subtracting decimals

When you add and subtract, estimate an approximate answer first.
To find an approximate answer, round to the nearest 10 or 1 to make the numbers easy to calculate in your head.

Example 1	Example 2
What is 364.74 added to 107.49?	What is 4.651 subtract 1.965?
An approximate answer is 360 + 110 = 470	An approximate answer is 5 − 2 = 3

Example 1:
$$3^16^14.^174$$
$$+\,1\ 0\ 7\,.\,4\ 9$$
$$\overline{4\ 7\ 2\,.\,2\ 3}$$

Example 2:
$$^34.^{15}6^{14}\cancel{5}\ ^11$$
$$-\,1\,.\,9\ \ 6\ \ 5$$
$$\overline{2\,.\,6\ \ 8\ \ 6}$$

1 Write approximate answers as whole numbers, then calculate the exact answer.

a)
$$5.658$$
$$+2.752$$

b)
$$13.27$$
$$+51.82$$

c)
$$5.903$$
$$+2.319$$

d)
$$412.79$$
$$+178.16$$

e)
$$61.58$$
$$-39.52$$

f)
$$496.91$$
$$-208.96$$

g)
$$9.417$$
$$-7.298$$

h)
$$30.42$$
$$-19.78$$

2 Read and answer these. Write an approximate answer and an exact answer.

a) Add 29.08 to 38.44.

b) What is the sum of 235.88 and 129.26?

c) Total 1.717 and 4.355.

d) What is 8.794 subtract 5.097?

e) What is the difference between 700.63 and 291.44?

f) What is 26.35 less than 56.183?

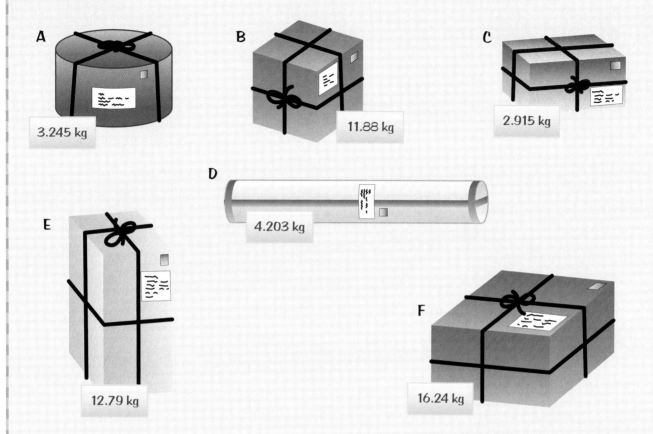

A 3.245 kg

B 11.88 kg

C 2.915 kg

D 4.203 kg

E 12.79 kg

F 16.24 kg

1 Write the parcels in order of weight, starting with the heaviest.

2 Round each weight to the nearest kilogram.

3 Round each weight to the nearest tenth of a kilogram.

4 Answer these.

   a) What is the total weight of parcels C and D?

   b) How much do parcel B and E weigh altogether?

   c) Parcel A and parcel C are carried together. What is the total weight being carried?

   d) What is the difference in weight between parcels F and B?

   e) How much more does parcel D weigh than parcel A?

   f) How much less does parcel E weigh than parcel F?

5 Answer these.

   a) Which two parcels have a total weight less than 7 kg?

   b) What is the total weight of parcel B, parcel E and parcel F?
      Write both the approximate weight and the exact weight.

   c) Which parcel weighs 0.33 kg less than parcel A?

   d) Which two parcels have a difference in weight of 0.91 kg?

Unit 2 Number properties

Rules of divisibility

Remember these rules of divisibility.
A whole number is divisible by, or can be divided exactly by:

2 if the last digit is even.	7 if you double the last digit and subtract it from the rest of the number, and the answer is 0 or divisible by 7.
3 if the sum of its digits can be divided by 3.	
4 if the last two digits can be divided by 4.	8 if the last three digits can be divided by 8.
5 if the last digit is 0 or 5.	9 if the sum of its digits is divisible by 9.
6 if it is even and the sum of its digits is divisible by 3.	10 if the last digit is 0.

1 Copy each sentence. Write the numbers 2, 3, 4, 5, 6, 7, 8, 9 or 10 in the correct boxes. Use the rules of divisibility to find the answers.

a) 1468 is divisible by ☐ and ☐

b) 2745 is divisible by ☐, ☐ and ☐

c) 6102 is divisible by ☐, ☐, ☐ and ☐

d) 24 096 is divisible by ☐, ☐, ☐, ☐ and ☐

e) 252 252 is divisible by ☐, ☐, ☐, ☐, ☐ and ☐

f) 456 030 is divisible by ☐, ☐, ☐, ☐, ☐ and ☐

g) 313 470 is divisible by ☐, ☐, ☐, ☐, ☐ and ☐

h) 151 200 is divisible by ☐, ☐, ☐, ☐, ☐, ☐, ☐, ☐ and ☐

2 Investigate these for divisibility by 2, 3, 4, 5, 6, 7, 8, 9 or 10.

a) What is the smallest number that is divisible by exactly 3 numbers?

b) What is the smallest number that is divisible by exactly 4 numbers?

c) What is the smallest number that is divisible by exactly 5 numbers?

d) What is the smallest number that is divisible by exactly 6 numbers?

3 Play the game of **'Three in a line'** on this grid.
It is a game for two players.

You need:
20 counters each
A blank dice with the numbers 3, 4, 5, 6, 8 and 9 written on it. Alternatively, write these six numbers on small pieces of paper to pick out of a bag.

60 480	21 480	7938	80 637	9515	25 848
14 256	7830	1944	68 295	41 961	37 290
3825	37 296	70 034	38 169	92 305	48 900
60 021	8292	43 120	21 945	9216	4707
93 145	71 004	24 135	39 252	7323	39 264
42 786	80 460	71 675	8365	12 888	9861

To play:
• Take turns to roll the dice, or pick a number from the bag.
• Choose a number on the grid that is divisible by the dice number.
• Place one of your counters on the number.

The aim is to place three counters in a line in any direction, vertically, horizontally or diagonally.
The first player to get three in a line is the winner.

Change the rules:
• Make it a **'Four in a line'** game.
• Roll two dice. Choose a number that is divisible by both dice numbers.

Multiples

Remember…
A multiple is a number made by multiplying together two other numbers.

$6 \times 8 = 48$, so 48 is a **common multiple** of both 6 and 8.

The **lowest** (or **least**) **common multiple (LCM)** of 6 and 8 is 24.

1 Find all the common multiples up to 120 for each pair of numbers.

    a) 5 and 4   **b)** 3 and 10   **c)** 7 and 9   **d)** 8 and 3

    e) 6 and 8   **f)** 10 and 7   **g)** 3 and 5   **h)** 4 and 9

2 Find all the common multiples up to 150 for each set of numbers.

    a) 3, 4 and 8   **b)** 5, 6 and 9   **c)** 6, 7 and 4   **d)** 3, 5 and 4

    e) 4, 9 and 18   **f)** 3, 10 and 12   **g)** 6, 5 and 15   **h)** 8, 9 and 12

3 Use your answers from question 2. Circle the lowest common multiple (LCM) for each set of numbers.

4 Copy this Venn diagram on a large piece of paper.
Write any 20 numbers on the diagram. There must be at least 3 numbers in each section.

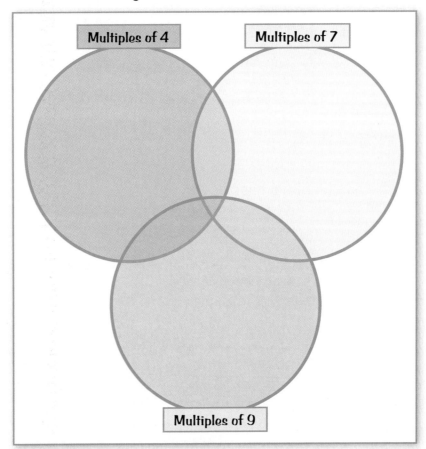

5 Find all the numbers in each box that are multiples of the centre number.

a)
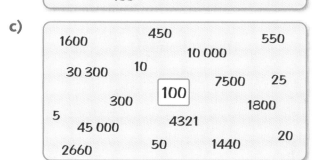

b)
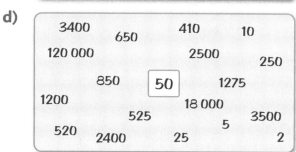

c)

31 130   40   1570
  20 202   1860
              60
195
     8080 **20** 1300   230
          320   10
1180   22 000 260
      100

125   250
     45   765
  815   5   1230
1975
    35   **25**   2000
       245   275
               8140
10 000   1055   25   225

c)
1600   450   550
       10 000
30 300 10
    300 **100** 7500 25
  5   1800
   45 000   4321
2660   50   1440   20

d)
3400   410   10
    650   2500
120 000   250
      850 **50** 1275
1200   18 000
       525   5 3500
520   2400   25   2

6 These numbers are joined by relationship arrows.

⟶ means 'is a multiple of'

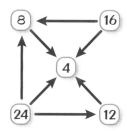

Copy and complete each set of numbers by drawing arrows.
It is important to get the direction of the arrows correct.

a)
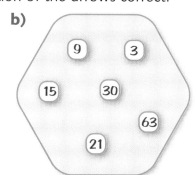

b)

c)
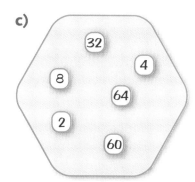

d) If the direction of the arrows in these were reversed, what would the relationship be?

Factors

Example 1
To find the common factors of 60, 15 and 45:
The factors of 60 are 1, 2, 3, 4, 5, 6, 10, 12, 15, 20, 30 and 60.
The factors of 15 are 1, 3, 5 and 15.
The factors of 45 are 1, 3, 5, 9, 15 and 45.
The common factors of 60, 15 and 45 are 1, 3, 5 and 15.
The **highest common factor (HCF)** is 15.

If a number only has two factors, itself and 1, then it is a **prime number**.
For example, 17 is a prime number because it can only be divided exactly by 1 and 17.
The number 1 is not a prime number because it only has one factor – itself.

The **prime factors** of a number are all those factors of the number which are themselves prime numbers. A prime number only has one prime factor – itself.

Example 2
All the factors of 12 are 1, 2, 3, 4, 6 and 12, but its only prime factors are 2 and 3.

1 Find the **common factors** for each of these.

a) 40 and 56

b) 35 and 80

c) 24 and 64

d) 90 and 115

e) 210 and 60

f) 42, 69 and 90

g) 112, 32 and 40

h) 42, 100 and 28

i) 64, 110 and 48

j) 90, 160 and 240

2 Use your answers from question 1. Circle the highest common factor (HCF) for each set of numbers.

One way to work out prime factors is to use factor trees.

Example

What are the prime factors of 36?

Start with any pair of factors of 36 and factorise them.
Continue until you get prime factors.

$3 \times 2 \times 2 \times 3 = 36$
$2^2 \times 3^2 = 36$
2 and 3 are prime factors of 36.

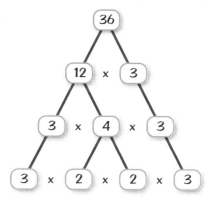

3 Copy and complete these factor trees.

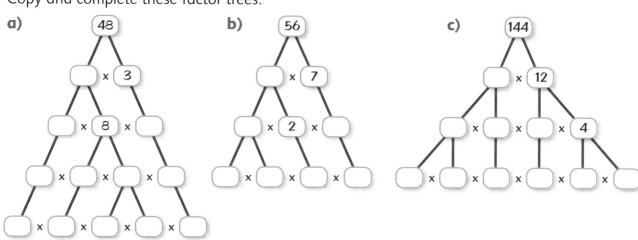

a) 48

b) 56

c) 144

4 Draw factor trees to find the prime factors of these numbers.

a) 42   b) 90   c) 72   d) 132

Try this

Look at this method for finding prime numbers.

	Example 1	Example 2
1. Think of a number	3	5
2. Multiply by 6	18	30
3. Subtract 1 from the answer	17	29
4. Add 1 to the answer	19	31
5. These are two prime numbers	17 and 19	29 and 31

Try this with other starting numbers to 50.
a) Which prime numbers can you find?
b) Which starting numbers does it not work for?
c) Which prime numbers are missing?

Squares, roots and powers

$1 \times 1 = 1$ 1 squared = 1 $1^2 = 1$	$2 \times 2 = 4$ 2 squared = 4 $2^2 = 4$	$3 \times 3 = 9$ 3 squared = 9 $3^2 = 9$	$4 \times 4 = 16$ 4 squared = 16 $4^2 = 16$

The numbers 1, 4, 9 and 16 are examples of **square numbers**, when two identical whole numbers are multiplied together.

On a calculator there is a $\sqrt{\ }$ key. This is called a square root key. The square root of a number is another number which, when squared, will equal the first number.

Examples
$\sqrt{9} = 3$ $\sqrt{36} = 5$

Remember…
$10 \times 10 \times 10 = 10^3 = 1000$

You sometimes need to multiply a number by itself lots of times.

$2 \times 2 \times 2 \times 2 = 16$

A quick way to write this is 2^4 (say this as '2 to the power of 4').

$2^4 = 16$ The small number 4 is the index and the 2 is the base.

1 Write square numbers for each of these.

a) 9^2 b) 7^2 c) 6^2 d) 8^2 e) 1^2

f) 25^2 g) 18^2 h) 32^2 i) 44^2 j) 120^2

2 Write the square root of each of these numbers.

a) $\sqrt{64}$ b) $\sqrt{36}$ c) $\sqrt{81}$ d) $\sqrt{144}$ e) $\sqrt{49}$

f) $\sqrt{100}$ g) $\sqrt{25}$ h) $\sqrt{121}$ i) $\sqrt{225}$ j) $\sqrt{900}$

3 Find the value of each of the following.

a) $35^2 + 28^2$ b) $154^2 - 92^2$ c) $180^2 + 133^2$

d) $271^2 - 170^2$ e) $222^2 + 241^2$ f) $356^2 - 355^2$

4 Write the value of these numbers.

a) $3^4 = (3 \times 3 \times 3 \times 3) =$

b) $2^3 = (2 \times 2 \times 2) =$

c) $10^3 = (10 \times 10 \times 10) =$

d) $2^5 = (2 \times 2 \times 2 \times 2 \times 2) =$

e) $5^4 = (5 \times 5 \times 5 \times 5) =$

f) $8^5 = (8 \times 8 \times 8 \times 8 \times 8) =$

5 Copy and complete this chart.

Power	Base	Index	Meaning	Numeral
4^2	4	2	4×4	16
2^4				
	6	3		
			$5 \times 5 \times 5 \times 5$	
10^5				
	3			81
			$9 \times 9 \times 9$	
	2			128

6 Write the answer for these.

a) What is 19^2?

b) What is the next square number after 144?

c) What is the square root of 361?

d) What is 11^4?

e) What is $\sqrt{2500}$?

f) What is 14 squared?

g) What is $\sqrt{1}$?

h) What is 2^{10}?

Try this

$12 = 4^2 - 2^2$

Twelve can be calculated by finding the difference between two square numbers.
Investigate which numbers from 1 to 50 can be made by calculating the difference between two square numbers.

Calculating square roots

Remember...
A square root is the opposite of a square number.
One way to calculate the square root is to divide the number by prime numbers until it is reduced to 1.

$\sqrt{484}$ = 484 ÷ 2   So, 484 = 2 × 2 × 11 × 11
    242 ÷ 2   = (2 × 11) × (2 × 11)
    121 ÷ 11   = 22 × 22
    11 ÷ 11 $\sqrt{484}$ = **22**
    1

1 Find the value of each of the following.

a) $\sqrt{576}$ b) $\sqrt{676}$ c) $\sqrt{841}$

d) $\sqrt{961}$ e) $\sqrt{1225}$ f) $\sqrt{1444}$

g) $\sqrt{1600}$ h) $\sqrt{8464}$ i) $\sqrt{6889}$

j) $\sqrt{12\,100}$ k) $\sqrt{31\,329}$ l) $\sqrt{45\,369}$

2 Find the value of each of the following.

a) $\sqrt{49} + \sqrt{100}$ b) $\sqrt{36} + \sqrt{169}$ c) $\sqrt{144} - \sqrt{25}$

d) $\sqrt{289} - \sqrt{121}$ e) $\sqrt{1024} + \sqrt{529}$ f) $\sqrt{900} - \sqrt{729}$

g) $\sqrt{1521} - \sqrt{1296}$ h) $\sqrt{324} \times \sqrt{256}$ i) $\sqrt{441} \times \sqrt{81}$

j) $\sqrt{900} \times \sqrt{400}$ k) $\sqrt{1156} - \sqrt{576}$ l) $\sqrt{3844} - \sqrt{2401}$

3 Some square roots do not have whole-number answers.

Estimate each of the following square roots.

a) $\sqrt{378}$ b) $\sqrt{294}$ c) $\sqrt{687}$

d) $\sqrt{162}$ e) $\sqrt{502}$ f) $\sqrt{921}$

g) $\sqrt{275}$ h) $\sqrt{236}$ i) $\sqrt{2400}$

j) $\sqrt{730}$ k) $\sqrt{469}$ l) $\sqrt{1300}$

4 Use a calculator to check your estimates in question 3.
Round your answers to the nearest tenth.

1 Is this statement always true, sometimes true, or never true?

   The product of the lowest common multiple (LCM) and highest common factor (HCF) of any two numbers is always equal to the product of those two numbers.

2 Which prime numbers less than 100 are also prime numbers when their digits are reversed?

3 3 and 5 are prime numbers. They are also consecutive odd numbers. Find how many pairs of consecutive odd numbers between 100 and 200 are both prime numbers.

4 Copy this grid.
   Write the values to complete the number puzzle.

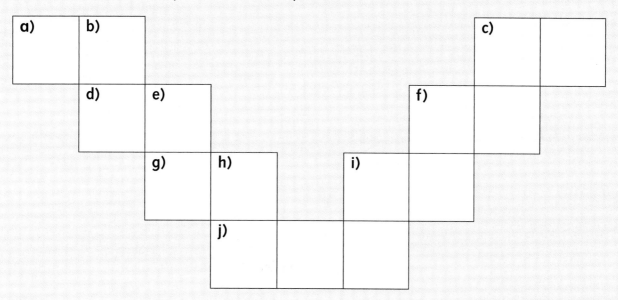

Across

a) One less than 7^2

c) $\sqrt{121}$

d) The HCF of 36 and 54

f) 6^2

g) 2^4

i) $\sqrt{144}$

j) 20^2

Down

b) 3^4

c) The HCF of 32 and 48

e) 9^2

f) 2^5

h) 8 squared

i) The LCM of 2 and 5

Unit 3 Fractions

Equivalent fractions

$\frac{1}{2} = \frac{2}{4} = \frac{3}{6} = \frac{4}{8} = \frac{5}{10}$ ... and so on.

These fractions are all equivalent. They are worth the same.

To reduce a fraction to its simplest form you divide the numerator and the denominator by the same number. This is sometimes called **cancelling** a fraction.

Example

What is $\frac{9}{21}$ reduced to its simplest form?

$\dfrac{9 \div 3 = 3}{21 \div 3 = 7}$

1 Copy and complete this chart of equivalent fractions.

Fraction	sixths	eighths	twelfths	twentieths	twenty-fourths
$\frac{1}{2}$	$\frac{3}{6}$	$\frac{4}{8}$	$\frac{6}{12}$	$\frac{10}{20}$	$\frac{12}{24}$
$\frac{2}{3}$	$\frac{4}{6}$				
$\frac{3}{4}$					
$\frac{1}{5}$					
$\frac{3}{5}$					
$\frac{5}{6}$					
$\frac{3}{8}$					
$\frac{7}{10}$					

2 Copy and complete these.

a) $\dfrac{3}{10} = \dfrac{\square}{20} = \dfrac{\square}{50} = \dfrac{27}{\square} = \dfrac{33}{\square} = \dfrac{\square}{150}$

b) $\dfrac{5}{8} = \dfrac{25}{\square} = \dfrac{40}{\square} = \dfrac{\square}{80} = \dfrac{\square}{96} = \dfrac{\square}{176}$

c) $\dfrac{120}{144} = \dfrac{\square}{72} = \dfrac{55}{\square} = \dfrac{25}{\square} = \dfrac{\square}{18} = \dfrac{\square}{6}$

d) $\dfrac{108}{198} = \dfrac{90}{\square} = \dfrac{\square}{99} = \dfrac{36}{\square} = \dfrac{\square}{44} = \dfrac{6}{\square}$

e) $\dfrac{24}{288} = \dfrac{12}{\square} = \dfrac{7}{\square} = \dfrac{\square}{60} = \dfrac{\square}{36} = \dfrac{1}{\square}$

3 Cancel each fraction to make it as simple as possible.

a) $\dfrac{60}{100}$ b) $\dfrac{16}{20}$ c) $\dfrac{30}{50}$ d) $\dfrac{12}{16}$

e) $\dfrac{85}{100}$ f) $\dfrac{18}{24}$ g) $\dfrac{12}{18}$ h) $\dfrac{24}{64}$

i) $\dfrac{24}{100}$ j) $\dfrac{64}{100}$ k) $\dfrac{35}{50}$ l) $\dfrac{64}{72}$

4 Two of each of these cancel down to the same fraction, but the other cancels down to a different fraction. Find the 'odd one out' for each set.

a) $\dfrac{9}{21}$ $\dfrac{4}{14}$ $\dfrac{15}{35}$

b) $\dfrac{48}{80}$ $\dfrac{30}{100}$ $\dfrac{21}{35}$

c) $\dfrac{14}{20}$ $\dfrac{19}{76}$ $\dfrac{14}{56}$

d) $\dfrac{12}{16}$ $\dfrac{10}{15}$ $\dfrac{18}{24}$

e) $\dfrac{22}{30}$ $\dfrac{121}{165}$ $\dfrac{60}{80}$

f) $\dfrac{81}{90}$ $\dfrac{60}{100}$ $\dfrac{36}{40}$

Try this

a) What is $\frac{1}{5}$ of 100?

b) $\dfrac{1}{5} = \dfrac{\square}{100}$

c) What do you notice about the two answers above?

d) Try this with $\frac{2}{5}$ and $\frac{3}{5}$ of 100. What happens?

e) Now try this with fifths of other numbers (make sure they are multiples of 5).

f) Can you write a rule to describe what happens?

g) Try other fractions with other numbers.

Comparing and ordering fractions

To compare and order any fractions you need to change them to equivalent fractions with a **common denominator**.
To do this you need to know the **lowest common multiple (LCM)** for each denominator.

Example
Which is the larger fraction, $\frac{5}{9}$ or $\frac{7}{12}$?

The LCM of 9 and 12 is 36.

$$\frac{5}{9} = \frac{20}{36} \qquad \frac{7}{12} = \frac{21}{36}$$

$\frac{21}{36} > \frac{20}{36}$ so $\frac{7}{12}$ is greater than $\frac{5}{9}$

1 Write < , > or = between each pair of fractions.
Remember to change them to equivalent fractions.

a) $\frac{1}{2} \square \frac{3}{7}$

b) $\frac{5}{6} \square \frac{7}{10}$

c) $\frac{5}{6} \square \frac{7}{8}$

d) $\frac{2}{11} \square \frac{1}{4}$

e) $\frac{3}{10} \square \frac{5}{12}$

f) $\frac{13}{24} \square \frac{8}{15}$

g) $\frac{33}{100} \square \frac{1}{3}$

h) $\frac{25}{36} \square \frac{17}{25}$

2 Find the common denominators for these fractions and write them in order, starting with the smallest. Then write the original fractions in order.

a) $\frac{5}{6} \qquad \frac{1}{3} \qquad \frac{5}{12} \qquad \frac{3}{4}$

b) $\frac{1}{4} \qquad \frac{3}{20} \qquad \frac{2}{5} \qquad \frac{3}{10}$

c) $\frac{2}{7} \qquad \frac{1}{5} \qquad \frac{3}{7} \qquad \frac{3}{5}$

d) $\frac{1}{2} \qquad \frac{5}{9} \qquad \frac{4}{9} \qquad \frac{2}{3}$

e) $\frac{1}{4} \qquad \frac{4}{15} \qquad \frac{2}{5} \qquad \frac{1}{3}$

f) $\frac{5}{8} \qquad \frac{4}{7} \qquad \frac{3}{4} \qquad \frac{3}{7}$

g) $\frac{1}{8} \qquad \frac{3}{25} \qquad \frac{2}{25} \qquad \frac{1}{12}$

h) $\frac{8}{11} \qquad \frac{3}{4} \qquad \frac{4}{5} \qquad \frac{2}{3}$

For this 'Field of fractions' activity, you will need a piece of squared paper.

a) Copy this coordinate grid.
Make sure you label the *x*-axis **denominator** and *y*-axis **numerator**.

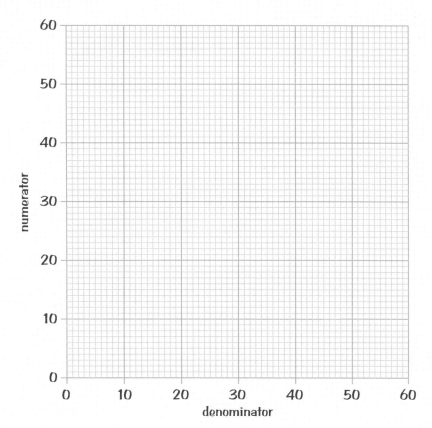

Each fraction is going to have a point on the grid.

For example, $\frac{1}{2}$ is at the point (2, 1), and $\frac{3}{5}$ is at the point (5, 3).

b) Plot the point for $\frac{1}{2}$ on the grid. Now plot points for all its equivalent fractions ($\frac{2}{4}$, $\frac{3}{6}$, $\frac{4}{8}$, …)

c) Join up the points. What do you notice?

d) Repeat this for other sets of equivalent fractions, such as $\frac{1}{4}$, $\frac{2}{5}$, $\frac{1}{3}$, $\frac{3}{4}$,…
Plot the points and join up each set.

e) Compare the fractions and write what you notice about the 'field of fractions' diagram.

f) How can the diagram help you decide when one fraction is bigger than another?

Adding and subtracting fractions

Fractions with different denominators are **unlike** fractions.
To add or subtract unlike fractions, we change them to **like** fractions by looking for equivalent fractions with a common denominator.

Example 1

Add $\frac{1}{4}$ and $\frac{3}{8}$

Common denominator is 8.

$$\frac{2}{8} + \frac{3}{8} = \frac{5}{8}$$

Example 2

Subtract $\frac{7}{10}$ from $\frac{5}{6}$

Common denominator is 30

$$\frac{25}{30} - \frac{21}{30} = \frac{4}{30} = \frac{2}{15}$$

1 Add these.
Cancel to write the answers in their simplest form if necessary.

a) $\frac{1}{3} + \frac{5}{12} =$

b) $\frac{2}{3} + \frac{2}{9} =$

c) $\frac{6}{25} + \frac{3}{5} =$

d) $\frac{1}{4} + \frac{1}{3} =$

e) $\frac{4}{5} + \frac{1}{11} =$

f) $\frac{1}{4} + \frac{1}{6} =$

g) $\frac{1}{8} + \frac{7}{12} =$

h) $\frac{4}{9} + \frac{3}{15} =$

i) $\frac{3}{4} + \frac{1}{30} =$

j) $\frac{17}{48} + \frac{1}{16} =$

k) $\frac{9}{35} + \frac{3}{10} =$

l) $\frac{1}{24} + \frac{7}{30} =$

2 Subtract these.
Cancel to write the answers in their simplest form if necessary.

a) $\frac{23}{24} - \frac{5}{8} =$

b) $\frac{19}{30} - \frac{3}{10} =$

c) $\frac{16}{25} - \frac{2}{5} =$

d) $\frac{7}{20} - \frac{33}{100} =$

e) $\frac{15}{32} - \frac{3}{8} =$

f) $\frac{5}{12} - \frac{11}{60} =$

g) $\frac{7}{8} - \frac{2}{3} =$

h) $\frac{1}{8} - \frac{1}{9} =$

i) $\frac{7}{12} - \frac{2}{7} =$

j) $\frac{11}{14} - \frac{3}{4} =$

k) $\frac{9}{10} - \frac{5}{6} =$

l) $\frac{16}{25} - \frac{11}{20} =$

3 Add together these fractions.

a) $\dfrac{1}{4}$ + $\dfrac{5}{12}$ + $\dfrac{1}{12}$

b) $\dfrac{3}{8}$ + $\dfrac{1}{12}$ + $\dfrac{1}{3}$

c) $\dfrac{1}{4}$ + $\dfrac{1}{3}$ + $\dfrac{1}{10}$ + $\dfrac{1}{12}$

d) $\dfrac{1}{3}$ + $\dfrac{1}{4}$ + $\dfrac{1}{5}$ + $\dfrac{1}{6}$

4 **a)** Draw four 4 × 4 squares on squared or spotty paper.

b) Draw straight lines to divide each grid into three unequal parts.

c) Divide each grid differently.

d) Write the fraction of each part.

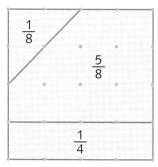

Try this

The ancient Egyptians only used fractions with a numerator of 1 (called unitary fractions). To make other fractions they added different unitary fractions to make the one they wanted.

Examples

$\dfrac{2}{3}$ would be written as $\dfrac{1}{2}$ + $\dfrac{1}{6}$

$\dfrac{7}{8}$ would be written as $\dfrac{1}{2}$ + $\dfrac{1}{4}$ + $\dfrac{1}{8}$

a) Add together ten or more pairs of unitary fractions with different denominators. Find out which fractions you can make in this way.

b) Explore making other fractions. Use as many unitary fractions as you like, but they must all have different denominators. Which fractions can you make with more than two fractions?

Improper fractions and mixed numbers

This circle is divided into 5 equal parts.

4 of the parts are shaded red.

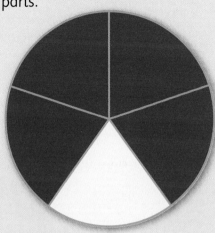

$\frac{4}{5}$

$4 \leftarrow$ The **numerator** tells you the number of those equal parts that are taken.

$5 \leftarrow$ The **denominator** tells you the number of equal parts the whole is divided into.

If the numerator is smaller than the denominator it is a **proper fraction**.

Example: $\frac{3}{8}$

If the numerator is larger than the denominator it is an **improper fraction**. It can also be written as a **mixed number**.

Example: $\frac{9}{4}$ or $2\frac{1}{4}$

Changing mixed numbers to improper fractions

Multiply the denominator by the whole number and then add the numerator.

Example:

$5\frac{3}{4} \rightarrow \square$

$(5 \times 4) + 3 = 23$ $5\frac{3}{4} = \frac{23}{4}$

Changing improper fractions to mixed numbers

Divide the numerator by the denominator to find how many whole numbers there are and any fractions remaining.

Example:

$\frac{27}{5} \rightarrow \square$

$\frac{27}{5} = 27 \div 5 = 5 \text{ r } 2$ $\frac{27}{5} = 5\frac{2}{5}$

1 Change these to mixed numbers or whole numbers.

a) $\frac{13}{4}$ b) $\frac{28}{3}$ c) $\frac{45}{7}$ d) $\frac{35}{6}$ e) $\frac{59}{2}$ f) $\frac{71}{8}$

2 Change these to improper fractions.

a) $7\frac{2}{5}$ b) $19\frac{3}{4}$ c) $8\frac{2}{9}$ d) $12\frac{1}{2}$ e) $11\frac{7}{12}$ f) $15\frac{3}{8}$

3 Add these together to make an improper fraction. Cancel if necessary and then write the answer as a mixed number.

a) $\frac{7}{21} + \frac{11}{12} =$ ☐

b) $\frac{3}{8} + \frac{15}{16} =$ ☐

c) $\frac{1}{2} + \frac{2}{3} =$ ☐

d) $\frac{3}{4} + \frac{5}{8} =$ ☐

e) $\frac{7}{10} + \frac{9}{20} =$ ☐

f) $\frac{2}{3} + \frac{3}{5} =$ ☐

4 Change the first fraction into an improper one, then subtract.

a) $1\frac{3}{8} - \frac{5}{8} =$ ☐

b) $1\frac{7}{20} - \frac{9}{20} =$ ☐

c) $1\frac{1}{3} - \frac{1}{2} =$ ☐

d) $1\frac{2}{5} - \frac{7}{10} =$ ☐

e) $1\frac{4}{7} - \frac{2}{3} =$ ☐

f) $1\frac{5}{6} - \frac{7}{8} =$ ☐

5 Add or subtract these mixed numbers.

a) $1\frac{5}{8} + 2\frac{1}{6} =$ ☐

b) $3\frac{2}{3} + 3\frac{3}{16} =$ ☐

c) $4\frac{7}{10} - 2\frac{3}{10} =$ ☐

d) $2\frac{1}{5} - 1\frac{1}{15} =$ ☐

e) $3\frac{2}{3} + 1\frac{3}{4} =$ ☐

f) $6\frac{1}{5} - 1\frac{8}{15} =$ ☐

g) $6\frac{5}{8} + 13\frac{13}{20} =$ ☐

h) $5\frac{3}{4} + 3\frac{7}{12} =$ ☐

i) $4\frac{9}{16} - 2\frac{29}{30} =$ ☐

Try this

a) Pick any mixed fraction. Add it to itself. | **Example** $3\frac{1}{4} + 3\frac{1}{4} = 6\frac{1}{2}$

b) What do you notice about the whole-number part and the fractional part?

c) Try this with five other mixed fractions. Is there a pattern in the results?

d) Look at the whole-number parts of your results. Some will be odd answers, some will be even. Can you work out why?

Fractions and percentages

Remember…
Percentages are simply fractions out of 100.
% is the percentage sign.
Some percentages are greater than 100%. $140\% = \frac{140}{100} = \frac{7}{5}$

To change fractions to percentages, find an equivalent fraction with the denominator 100. **Example 1** $\frac{4}{5} = \frac{80}{100} = 80\%$	To change percentages to fractions, write the percentage as a fraction out of 100 and then simplify. **Example 2** 30% is $\frac{30}{100}$, which is the same as $\frac{3}{10}$
Example 3 What percentage of 20 is 7? $\frac{7}{20} = \frac{(7 \times 5)}{(20 \times 5)} = \frac{35}{100}$ So, 7 is 35% of 20.	**Example 4** What percentage of 40 kg is 8 kg? $\frac{8}{40} = \frac{1}{5} = \frac{(1 \times 20)}{(5 \times 20)} = \frac{20}{100}$ So, 8 kg is 20% of 40 kg.

1 Write each of these fractions as a percentage.

a) $\frac{4}{5}$ b) $\frac{9}{10}$ c) $\frac{16}{20}$ d) $\frac{11}{25}$

e) $\frac{1}{4}$ f) $\frac{47}{50}$ g) $\frac{12}{5}$ h) $\frac{13}{10}$

i) $\frac{32}{25}$ j) $\frac{28}{40}$ k) $\frac{23}{4}$ l) $\frac{128}{25}$

m) $\frac{21}{12}$ n) $\frac{18}{30}$ o) $\frac{28}{35}$ p) $\frac{51}{68}$

2 Write each of these percentages as a fraction reduced to its simplest form.

a) 34%   b) 76%   c) 51%   d) 48%

e) 24%   f) 38%   g) 15%   h) 18%

i) 175%   j) 284%   k) 29%   l) 645%

m) 128%   n) 385%   o) 420%   p) 135%

3 The first number or amount is what percentage of the second number or amount?

a) 3 and 10   b) 5 and 25   c) 6 and 20

d) 1 kg and 4 kg   e) 16 and 40   f) 7 litres and 10 litres

g) 45 m and 50 m   h) 25 kg and 100 kg   i) 170 m and 500 m

j) 350 g and 1 kg   k) 400 m and 1 km   l) 80 ml and 400 ml

Investigate what percentage of the numbers on a 1 to 100 number square are:

a) odd numbers

b) multiples of 3

c) multiples of 2 and 5

d) square numbers

e) factors of 36.

1	2	3	4	5	6	7	8	9	10
11	12	13	14	15	16	17	18	19	20
21	22	23	24	25	26	27	28	29	30
31	32	33	34	35	36	37	38	39	40
41	42	43	44	45	46	47	48	49	50
51	52	53	54	55	56	57	58	59	60
61	62	63	64	65	66	67	68	69	70
71	72	73	74	75	76	77	78	79	80
81	82	83	84	85	86	87	88	89	90
91	92	93	94	95	96	97	98	99	100

Assessment

Look at this set of fractions.

$$\frac{14}{20} \qquad \frac{9}{15} \qquad \frac{16}{40} \qquad \frac{24}{32} \qquad \frac{18}{27}$$

1 Reduce each fraction and write it in its simplest form.

2 Write the fractions in order, starting with the smallest.

3 Answer these.

    a) What is the total of the two largest fractions?

    b) What is the difference between the largest and smallest fractions?

    c) Which two fractions total $1\frac{4}{15}$?

    d) Which two fractions have a difference of $\frac{3}{10}$?

4 Write each of the fractions as a percentage.

Unit 4 Assess and review

Integers and review

1 What is the difference between −8 and 9?

    a) −1   **b)** 1   **c)** 17

2 What is the value of the red digit in 0.1783?

    a) $\frac{3}{1000}$ **b)** $\frac{3}{10\,000}$ **c)** 3000

3 Which number is 11×10^3?

    a) 11 000   **b)** 1100   **c)** 111 000

4 What is 29.664 09 rounded to the nearest tenth?

    a) 29.6   **b)** 29.66   **c)** 29.7

5 Which integers could go in the boxes?

    a) $-9 \leq \square \leq -5$ **b)** $-7 \leq \square \leq 1$ **c)** $-22 \leq \square \leq -17$ **d)** $-3 \leq \square \leq 4$

    e) $0 \geq \square \geq -4$ **f)** $-5 \geq \square \geq -8$ **g)** $2 \geq \square \geq -2$ **h)** $-26 \geq \square \geq -30$

6 Answer these.
    a) The temperature is −4°C. It rises by 8 degrees and then drops by 3 degrees. What is the temperature now?
    b) The temperature is 2°C. It falls by 9 degrees and then drops a further 4 degrees. What is the temperature now?
    c) The temperature is −5°C. It falls by 6 degrees and then rises by 2 degrees. What is the temperature now?

7 This table shows ten countries of the world that have large populations.
Copy and complete the table.

Country	Population	a) Round to the nearest 100	b) Round to the nearest 1000	c) Round to the nearest 10 000
Brazil	187 078 227			
China	1 323 973 713			
Egypt	75 887 007			
India	1 135 351 995			
Iran	71 288 433			
Japan	127 763 611			
Nigeria	148 059 731			
Pakistan	164 803 560			
Russia	142 093 540			
United States	304 176 035			

8 Write the countries from question 7 in order of population, starting with the largest.

9 Use these four digits and a decimal point to answer these.
There must be one digit in front of the decimal point.

a) What is the largest decimal number you can make?
b) What the smallest decimal number you can make?
c) Make a decimal number as near as possible to 2.5.
d) Make a decimal number as near as possible to 8.5.
e) Make a decimal number between 2.35 and 2.38.
f) Write all the decimal numbers you have made in order, from smallest to largest.

Try this

This is a **super-square**.

	× 10		
	7	70	700
÷ 10	0.7	7	70
	0.07	0.7	7

Copy and complete these super-squares.

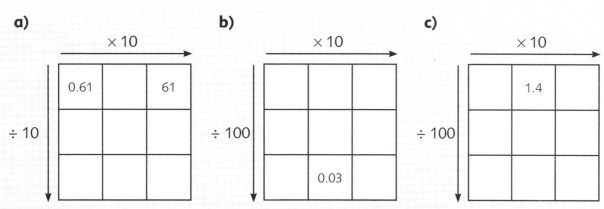

a)

	× 10	
0.61		61

÷ 10

b)

	× 10	
	0.03	

÷ 100

c)

	× 10	
	1.4	

÷ 100

Make up some of your own super-squares.

Number properties

1 What is $\sqrt{144}$?

   a) 18   **b)** 72   **c)** 12

2 Which of these is the lowest common multiple of 9 and 12?

   a) 54   **b)** 72   **c)** 36

3 Which of these numbers is the highest common factor of 28 and 35?

   a) 5   **b)** 7   **c)** 9

4 What is 2^5?

   a) 10   **b)** 32   **c)** 64

5 Copy these as large Venn diagrams.
Write the numbers 1 to 30 in each diagram.

   a) A → Prime numbers
       B → Odd numbers

   b) A → Square numbers
       B → Multiples of 3

   c) A → Factors of 72
       B → Factors of 60

   d) A → Multiples of 6
       B → Factors of 90

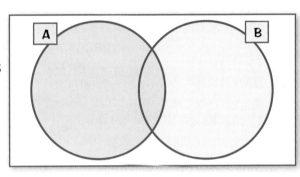

6 24 can be written as a product of prime factors.

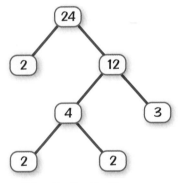

$24 = 2 \times 2 \times 2 \times 3$

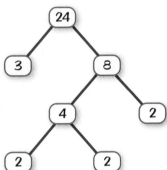

$24 = 3 \times 2 \times 2 \times 2$

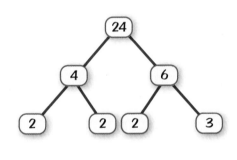

$24 = 2 \times 2 \times 2 \times 3$

The answers are all the same.

Write these numbers as products of their prime factors.

   a) 42   **b)** 28   **c)** 32   **d)** 48   **e)** 68   **f)** 36

7 Two prime numbers are added together. The answer is 100.
Find all the possible solutions.

8 Find the smallest number with exactly 3 factors.
Now find the smallest number with exactly 4 factors.
Continue this, finding the smallest number with 5, 6, 7, … factors.

9 What is the value of each of these?

   a) 9^2 **b)** 16^2 **c)** 28^2 **d)** 43^2 **e)** 57^2 **f)** 75^2

10 Calculate the value of each of these.

a) $8^2 + 72^2$

b) $18^2 - 13^2$

c) $26^2 - 20^2$

d) $395^2 - 219^2$

e) $444^2 - 188^2$

f) $492^2 + 327^2$

Try this

Write the following numbers on small squares of paper.

$\boxed{1}$ $\boxed{3}$ $\boxed{5}$ $\boxed{7}$ $\boxed{9}$

$\boxed{2}$ $\boxed{4}$ $\boxed{6}$ $\boxed{8}$

Place the numbers on this grid to make it true.

	Prime number	Common factor of 36 and 12	Factor of 72
Factor of 30			
Odd number			
Factor of 24			

Fractions

1 What is $\frac{13}{25}$ as a percentage?

   a) 13%   **b)** 42%   **c)** 52%

2 What is 45% as a fraction in its lowest terms?

   a) $\frac{4}{5}$ **b)** $\frac{3}{8}$ **c)** $\frac{9}{20}$

3 What is $\frac{1}{8} + \frac{7}{12}$?

   a) $\frac{2}{5}$ **b)** $\frac{7}{20}$ **c)** $\frac{17}{24}$

4 What is $2\frac{2}{5}$ subtract $1\frac{1}{6}$?

   a) $1\frac{7}{30}$ **b)** $1\frac{1}{11}$ **c)** $1\frac{13}{30}$

5 Basel investigates the set of proper fractions with the denominator 9.

$$\frac{1}{9} \qquad \frac{2}{9} \qquad \frac{{}^1\cancel{3}}{\cancel{9}_3} \qquad \frac{4}{9} \qquad \frac{5}{9} \qquad \frac{{}^2\cancel{6}}{\cancel{9}_3} \qquad \frac{7}{9} \qquad \frac{8}{9}$$

He circles the ones that could be cancelled to a simpler form.

   a) Investigate the sets of fractions with denominators 10, 11, 12, 13, … up to 20.

   b) Which sets have no fractions that can be cancelled?

   c) What can you say about their denominators?

6 Copy and complete these.

a)

+	$\frac{1}{6}$	$\frac{5}{6}$	$\frac{3}{8}$	$\frac{2}{9}$
$\frac{1}{3}$	$\frac{1}{2}$			
$\frac{1}{4}$				
$\frac{5}{6}$				
$\frac{7}{8}$				

b)

+	$1\frac{4}{5}$	$1\frac{1}{8}$	$2\frac{3}{4}$	$3\frac{2}{3}$
$\frac{2}{5}$				
$\frac{1}{8}$				
$\frac{3}{5}$				
$\frac{7}{10}$				

7 Copy and complete each of these fractions and percentages.

   a) $\frac{3}{5} = \boxed{}$ %   **b)** $\frac{47}{50} = \boxed{}$ %   **c)** $\frac{7}{2} = \boxed{}$ %   **d)** $\frac{42}{25} = \boxed{}$ %

   e) 65% $= \boxed{}$ **f)** 92% $= \boxed{}$ **g)** 105% $= \boxed{}$ **h)** 225% $= \boxed{}$

8 The first number or amount is what percentage of the second number or amount?

   a) $9 and $20   **b)** 8 kg and 25 kg   **c)** 17 litres and 50 litres

   d) 12 kg and 10 kg   **e)** $150 and $50   **f)** 45 m and 50 m

Play **'Fraction frenzy'** in pairs or small groups.

You need:
1 to 8 number cards

To play:

Player 1
• Shuffle the cards and pick out any four numbers.
• Arrange them to make a fraction addition.
• Work out the answer to the calculation.

$$\frac{\Box}{\Box} + \frac{\Box}{\Box} = \Box$$

Player 2
• Shuffle all the cards again and pick out any four numbers.
• Use the four numbers to make a fraction subtraction.
• Work out the answer to the calculation.

$$\frac{\Box}{\Box} - \frac{\Box}{\Box} = \Box$$

Target:
• The aim is for Player 2 to make an answer that is the same, or as close as possible, to the answer made by Player 1.
• Set a time limit of 3 minutes to arrange the cards.

Points are scored as follows:

Exact match	Less than $\frac{1}{10}$ difference	Less than $\frac{1}{5}$ difference	Less than $\frac{1}{2}$ difference
10 points	5 points	3 points	1 point

Take turns to start and play each other four times to find the winner.

Addition and subtraction of whole numbers

When you use a written method to add or subtract numbers, remember to line up each number carefully. Always estimate an approximate answer first.

Example 1

What is the total of 455 682, 376 067 and 218 129?

Estimate:

460 000 + 380 000 + 220 000 → 1 060 000

```
  ¹4 ¹5 5  ¹6 ¹8 2
     3 7 6   0 6 7
  +  2 1 8   1 2 9
  ─────────────────
  1 0 4 9   8 7 8
```

Example 2

What is 684 508 subtract 192 364?

Estimate:

680 000 – 190 000 → 490 000

```
  ⁵6̸ ¹8 4  ⁴5̸ ¹0 8
  – 1 9 2   3 6 4
  ─────────────────
    4 9 2   1 4 4
```

1 For each of the following calculations, estimate the answer then work it out. When you have worked out the answer, check it against your estimate.

a)
```
    6 1 2  8 5 3
  + 2 1 5  6 3 3
```

b)
```
    3 6 8  1 0 6
  + 2 5 8  6 4 2
```

c)
```
    7 5 3  1 5 9
  + 6 4 5  1 1 3
```

d)
```
    8 7 4  5 5 1
  + 3 2 9  9 6 2
```

e)
```
    2 4 1  3 3 2
    8 4 4  5 6 3
  + 8 8 7  4 5 3
```

f)
```
    7 5 6  0 8 5
    3 1 1  2 5 8
  + 1 4 8  6 5 2
```

g)
```
    9 8 5  4 5 4
    6 6 5  4 1 2
    6 7 4  5 6 4
  + 2 3 3  0 0 1
```

h)
```
    9 4 5  2 2 3
    6 3 5  6 4 1
    3 3 2  1 1 1
  + 7 5 1  5 6 1
```

i)
```
     6 5  3 5 2
    3 4 1  5 5 9
         2 4 8
       1 6 5 7
  +      4 8 8
```

j)
```
    3 6  5 4 1
       6 4 4 2
         9 5 4
         5 4 5
  +    7 5 5 6
```

k)
```
       6 5 4 2
    8 7 5  4 4 5
     6 5  4 4 8
         5 5 7
  +  1 2  6 8 8
```

l)
```
     6 8  6 4 5
    2 2 3  6 6 7
       5 2 6 3
       7 5 4 4
  + 5 8 4  6 6 5
```

2 Answer these.

a) 413 521 + 238 604 + 52 632 175 + 1 654 885 =

b) 365 709 + 331 992 + 6 523 831 + 41 912 563 + 560 523 =

c) 108 802 + 3 315 267 + 252 996 + 3 296 256 + 98 330 851 =

d) 1 618 145 + 5 246 374 + 36 352 + 92 987 546 + 179 044 =

3 For each of the following calculations, estimate the answer then work it out.
When you have worked out the answer, check it against your estimate.

a)
```
  5 6 5 3 4 1
- 1 2 5 6 4 1
```

b)
```
  8 4 5 1 7
-   5 4 0 8 4
```

c)
```
  9 4 8 6 8 5
- 4 8 0 4 8 7
```

d)
```
  8 7 5 6 4 5
- 5 8 4 5 0 5
```

e)
```
  8 4 5 6 5 2
- 2 5 1 0 8 6
```

f)
```
  9 8 6 4 5
-   3 7 5 4 2
```

g)
```
  7 4 1 8 5 2
- 2 5 8 1 4 7
```

h)
```
  9 5 1 7 5 3
- 3 5 7 1 5 9
```

i)
```
  2 1 4 6 5 8 2
-   3 5 4 9 7 8
```

j)
```
  3 5 4 2 0 8 7
-   5 9 7 5 0 4
```

k)
```
  6 5 8 4 6 5 2
-   7 6 6 2 7 1
```

l)
```
  2 8 6 4 5 2 8
-   7 6 5 9 7 8
```

4 Answer these.

a) 59 865 674 − 32 598 665 =

b) 91 445 263 − 51 308 674 =

c) 863 125 671 − 1 981 664 =

d) 29 862 953 − 1 102 140 =

e) 54 228 653 − 4 071 269 =

f) 318 652 336 − 18 005 049 =

Try this

0 1 2 3 4 5 6 7 8 9

```
    5 1 4 0 8
+   6 3 2 7 9
  1 1 4 6 8 7
```

Use all the digits 0–9 to make a calculation with an answer between 100 000 and 120 000.

a) How close can you get to 100 000?

b) How close can you get to 120 000?

Addition and subtraction problems

If you have a word problem to solve, it may help to follow these stages:

Step 1 Read the problem. *Try to picture the problem and imagine going through it in real life.*	**Step 2** Sort out the calculations. *Is it an addition or subtraction or more than one calculation?*
Step 3 Answer the calculations. *Use a written or mental method.*	**Step 4** Answer the problem. *Look back at the question – what is it asking?*

1 Answer these.

    a) During December at an airport, 305 722 passengers travelled through Terminal 1 and 395 184 passengers travelled through Terminal 2.
How many passengers altogether travelled through Terminals 1 and 2?

    b) 608 910 bags passed through the airport. 496 190 were checked in to be loaded on the aircraft, the rest were hand luggage. How many bags were taken as hand luggage?

    c) There were 101 484 flights into Terminals 1 and 2 and another 137 969 flights into Terminal 3 in one year. How many flights were there in total at the airport?

    d) Terminal 1 can handle up to 6 526 300 passengers a year and Terminal 2 can take a maximum of 3 514 500 passengers a year. With the new Terminal 3 the airport can take a total of 22 851 200 passengers in a year using all three terminals.
How many passengers can Terminal 3 take in a year?

2 This chart shows how many cups of coffee were sold at the airport in February.

February	Week 1	Week 2	Week 3	Week 4
Cups of coffee	277 823	268 205	314 419	195 356

    a) How many cups of coffee were sold in the first two weeks?

    b) How many more cups of coffee were sold in week 3 than in week 4?

    c) How many cups of coffee were sold in total over the four weeks?

    d) At the start of the month a shop had enough coffee for 570 468 cups. They bought coffee for another 650 000 cups during the second week.
How many cups of coffee were left at the end of the month?

3 These tables show some information about agriculture in Egypt.

Agriculture	Annual production (tonnes)
Cereals	21 315 038
Meat	1 437 843
Fruit and vegetables	24 105 384
Root crops	2 938 076
Beans	483 216
Sugar crops	19 091 237
Milk	4 501 275

Resources	
Arable land (hectares)	2 801 306
Cattle (per head)	8 214 369
Sheep and goats (per head)	8 932 145

Use the tables to answer these.

a) How many tonnes of cereal and root crops are produced in total?

b) What is the weight difference between the meat production and the production of fruit and vegetables?

c) How many tonnes of milk and sugar are produced in total?

d) What is the total number of cattle, sheep and goats in Egypt?

e) How many more sheep and goats are there than cattle?

f) What is the difference in weight between the production of root crops and beans?

g) The total land area of Egypt is 99 545 186 hectares. What area of Egypt is not for arable use?

h) The total weight of production of root crops, beans and sugar crops is less than the total weight of fruit and vegetable produced. How much less?

i) The total weight of production of root crops, beans and sugar crops is more than the total weight of cereal produced. How much more?

Try this

Investigate to find out the population of Egypt. How many more people are there in Egypt than the total number of cattle, sheep and goats?

Order of operations: + , –, × and ÷

If a calculation involves more than one operation, it must be done in the following order:

DIVISION
↓
MULTIPLICATION
↓
ADDITION
↓
SUBTRACTION

Example 1
$9 \times 6 - 80 \div 10 = 72 - 8$
$= 64$

Example 2
$112 - 36 + 55 - 102 = 112 + 55 - 36 - 102$
$= 167 - 36 - 102$
$= 29$

1 Copy and complete these addition and subtraction calculations. Show all your working.

a) $36 - 47 - 92 + 124 =$
b) $75 - 46 + 31 - 28 =$
c) $89 - 23 - 17 - 36 =$

d) $75 - 149 + 23 + 84 =$
e) $7 - 62 - 182 + 321 =$
f) $86 + 17 - 99 + 16 =$

g) $53 - 24 + 48 - 67 =$
h) $92 - 23 - 68 - 88 + 139 =$
i) $142 - 86 - 21 - 17 =$

j) $436 + 69 - 256 - 127 =$
k) $67 - 342 - 167 + 623 =$
l) $36 + 57 + 321 - 297 =$

m) $57 - 69 - 148 - 231 + 406 =$
n) $246 - 45 - 192 - 9 =$
o) $274 + 38 - 527 + 463 =$

2 How many different answers can you get by placing the + or – sign in each diamond?

a) 28 16 23 =

b) 47 19 23 36 =

c) 112 67 87 132 =

3 Copy and complete.

a) $15 + 9 \times 3 =$
b) $43 - 27 \div 3 =$
c) $9 \times 8 + 15 =$

d) $54 \div 6 - 5 =$
e) $5 \times 6 - 14 =$
f) $56 - 3 \times 7 =$

g) $23 + 63 \div 7 =$
h) $89 - 88 \div 11 =$
i) $12 - 15 \div 3 + 9 =$

j) $15 + 8 \times 5 - 21 =$
k) $54 \div 9 + 32 - 17 =$
l) $42 - 3 \times 5 + 7 =$

m) $16 + 81 \div 9 + 36 =$
n) $87 - 55 + 6 \times 8 =$
o) $6 \times 7 - 32 + 74 =$

p) $18 \div 6 + 4 \times 7 =$
q) $9 \times 7 - 75 \div 5 =$
r) $120 \div 10 + 17 \times 2 =$

4 Copy and complete.

a) $43 \times 16 + 224 =$

b) $31 - 34 \div 8 =$

c) $132 - 13 \times 7 =$

d) $134 \div 5 + 87 =$

e) $137 \times 7 - 683 =$

f) $824 \div 32 + 369 =$

g) $226 - 897 \div 26 =$

h) $55 + 135 \div 6 =$

i) $947 - 43 \times 17 =$

j) $73 \times 34 + 29 =$

k) $79 \times 84 - 1278 =$

l) $89 + 12 \times 137 =$

m) $903 \div 35 + 169 =$

n) $65 \times 47 - 2723 =$

o) $762 + 43 \times 15 =$

p) $745 - 2295 \div 34 =$

q) $9585 \div 142 + 187 =$

r) $4787 - 29 \times 83 =$

Try this

Different calculators can give different answers to mixed operations.

$2 + 5 \times 3 \rightarrow 17$ $2 + 5 \times 3 \rightarrow 21$

Can you see how they work the calculations out?

Look back at questions 3 and 4. Use a calculator to check your answers.
Think carefully about the order of operations.

Brackets

If a calculation involves brackets, it must be done in the following order:

BRACKETS

$\downarrow$

DIVISION

$\downarrow$

MULTIPLICATION

$\downarrow$

ADDITION

$\downarrow$

SUBTRACTION

Example 1
$5 \times (3 + 8) - 2$
$= 5 \times 11 - 2$
$= 55 - 2$
$= 53$

Example 2
$(6 \times 2 - 8) + (12 \div 4 + 10)$
$= (12 - 8) + (3 + 10)$
$= 4 + 13$
$= 17$

1 Answer these.

a) $(7 \times 4) - 25$

b) $35 + (8 \times 6)$

c) $(49 \div 7) + 66$

d) $98 - (64 \div 2)$

e) $(13 \times 2) + (25 \div 5)$

f) $(85 \div 5) - (72 \div 8)$

g) $(25 \times 5) - (48 \times 2)$

h) $(23 + 32) \div (32 - 27)$

i) $(57 - 33) \times (73 - 69)$

j) $(87 - 73) \times (97 - 87)$

k) $(8 \times 7) \div (43 - 15)$

l) $(43 + 38) \div (27 \div 3)$

m) $(72 \div 8) \times (54 \div 9)$

n) $(76 \div 2 + 8) - (7 \times 7 - 3)$

o) $(7 \times 8 - 23) \div (9 \times 8 - 69)$

p) $99 - (9 \times 9)$

q) $(6 \times 9) + (6 \times 7)$

r) $(93 + 37) \div (43 - 38)$

2 Answer these.

a) $24 \times (14 + 8) - 50$

b) $(23 \times 14) + (12 \times 17)$

c) $(70 \times 72) \div (607 - 595)$

d) $(26 + 86) + (35 \times 8)$

e) $(351 \div 3) + (142 - 85)$

f) $243 + (172 + 278) \div 25$

g) $1000 - 7 \times (18 \times 7)$

h) $45 + 16 \times (137 - 112)$

i) $(37 \times 25) + (68 \div 4)$

j) $(28 \times 35) - (185 \div 5)$

k) $(5 \times 128) \div (47 - 39)$

l) $(846 \div 3) + (114 \div 6)$

3 Answer these. Remember to convert measures to the same unit.

a) $875\,g \times 98\% - 0.45\,kg = \boxed{}\,g$

b) $345\,g \times 112 - 24.3\,kg = \boxed{}\,kg$

c) $13.63\,l + 46.3\,cl - 34\,ml \times 392 = \boxed{}\,ml$

d) $(4.36\,kg + 270\,g) \times 154 = \boxed{}\,kg$

e) $(43.63\,ml - 5.75\,ml) \times 7500 = \boxed{}\,litres$

f) $105\,m - 7490\,cm \times 14 = \boxed{}\,m$

g) $361.9\,cm \div 8.8 + 38.75\,mm = \boxed{}\,cm$

h) $4.42\,l \div 1.25 - 270.4\,cl = \boxed{}\,ml$

i) $654\,g + 74.82\,kg \div 645 = \boxed{}\,kg$

j) $19.2 \times (27.8\,kg - 17.2\,kg) - 25.86\,kg = \boxed{}\,kg$

4 Copy and write in brackets to make these true.

a) $1.1 - 0.3 + 10 \times 0.02 = 1$

b) $1.5 + 0.21 \div 0.7 - 0.8 = 1$

c) $5.6 \div 7 + 2.3 - 2.1 = 1$

d) $0.2 \times 0.4 + 2.3 \times 0.4 = 1$

e) $0.85 + 1.05 - 8.1 \div 9 = 1$

Try this

Using only the digits 2, 4, 5, 7 and 9 and any operation ($+$, $-$, $\times$, $\div$), make each of the numbers below. Can you find different ways to make these numbers? Don't forget to use brackets.

a) 41   b) 59   c) 93   d) 87   e) 120

BODMAS

BODMAS is an acronym that helps you to remember the order for working out mixed operations.

1st	**B**	BRACKETS	( )
2nd	**O**	OF	Power of – e.g. 3^2
3rd	**D**	DIVISION	$\div$
4th	**M**	MULTIPLICATION	$\times$
5th	**A**	ADDITION	$+$
6th	**S**	SUBTRACTION	$-$

1 Answer these.

a) $110 - 7^2 + 22 \div 2$

b) $9 \times (8^2 - 15)$

c) $5 \times 8 - (17 + 8) \div 5$

d) $3 + 6 \times 4^2$

e) $(3 \times 8) + (7^2 \times 4)$

f) $75 \div 3 + (6 \times 9^2)$

g) $(24 - 20) \times 6 \div 3 + 7^2$

h) $3 + 6 \times 4^3 - 5$

i) $25^2 - (8^3 - 3)$

j) $(3^3 - 3^2) \times (7^2 - 2^3)$

2 Work out the missing numbers.

a) $(135 \div \boxed{}) + 3 = 30$

b) $(420 \div \boxed{}) - 5 = 65$

c) $(\boxed{} + 15) \times 8 = 640$

d) $(7 \times \boxed{}) - 55 = 155$

e) $(\boxed{} \div 5) + 25 = 75$

f) $(50 \times \boxed{}) + 18 = 218$

g) $(\boxed{} \div 3) - 65 = 35$

h) $(\boxed{} - 15) \times 7 = 210$

3 Copy these statements, using <, > or = to make each one true.

a) $(4^2 \times 5^2) + (12^2 \div 4^2) \boxed{} (8^2 + 6^2) + (3^2 \times 2^3)$

b) $2^4 + (8 \times 2^2) - 4^2 \boxed{} (4^2 \times 5) - (3^2 \times 4)$

c) $(14 \times 6) - (8^2 \div 4) + 8^2 \boxed{} 6^2 \times (180 \div 30) - 4^3$

d) $8^2 + (6^2 - 4) \times (7^2 - 38) \boxed{} 9^2 \times (3^2 + 7) + (3^3 \times 2^3)$

Rewrite each of these, using brackets to make the largest possible answer.

a) $14 + 8^2 - 5 \times 3^2$

b) $3 \times 190 - 11^2 + 15$

c) $10^2 \div 2 + 3^2 \times 70$

d) $6^2 - 2^2 \times 8^2 + 20$

Assessment

1 This chart shows the number of people visiting a large shopping mall each month for five months.

February	1 004 593
March	1 392 568
April	1 320 059
May	1 425 770
June	1 328 045

a) How many visitors were there in total in March and April?

b) How many more visitors were there in March than in June?

c) In July there were 93 268 fewer visitors than in June.
How many more visitors did they have in May than in July?

d) How many visitors were there in total over the six months?

2 Work these out.

a) $30 \times (12 + 17) - 38$

b) $(21 \times 18) + (11 \times 14)$

c) $(9^2 - 63) \times (7^2 - 22)$

d) $(2^3 + 19) - (75 \div 25)$

e) $(248 \div 2^2) + (95 - 18)$

f) $19^2 - (8^2 + 5^2) - 14$

Unit 6 Multiplication

Multiplying by a two-digit number

Remember to estimate an answer before multiplying.

Example

584 × 46

Estimate:
≈ 600 × 50
= 30 000

```
      584
    × 40
    ─────
    20 000   (500 × 40)
     3 200   ( 80 × 40)
       160   (  4 × 40)
     3 000   (500 ×  6)
       480   ( 80 ×  6)
        24   (  4 ×  6)
    ─────
    26 864
```

leading to

```
      584
    × 46
    ─────
    23 360   (584 × 40)
     3 504   (584 ×  6)
    ─────
    26 864
```

1 For each of the following calculations, estimate the answer then work it out. When you have worked out the answer, check it against your estimate.

a) $\begin{array}{r} 59 \\ \times\ 58 \\ \hline \end{array}$

b) $\begin{array}{r} 48 \\ \times\ 79 \\ \hline \end{array}$

c) $\begin{array}{r} 78 \\ \times\ 25 \\ \hline \end{array}$

d) $\begin{array}{r} 36 \\ \times\ 54 \\ \hline \end{array}$

e) $\begin{array}{r} 41 \\ \times\ 19 \\ \hline \end{array}$

f) $\begin{array}{r} 856 \\ \times\ 62 \\ \hline \end{array}$

g) $\begin{array}{r} 329 \\ \times\ 84 \\ \hline \end{array}$

h) $\begin{array}{r} 203 \\ \times\ 74 \\ \hline \end{array}$

i) $\begin{array}{r} 845 \\ \times\ 16 \\ \hline \end{array}$

j) $\begin{array}{r} 405 \\ \times\ 55 \\ \hline \end{array}$

2 For each of the following calculations, estimate the answer then work it out. When you have worked out the answer, check it against your estimate.

a) $\begin{array}{r} 5567 \\ \times\ 42 \\ \hline \end{array}$

b) $\begin{array}{r} 8561 \\ \times\ 36 \\ \hline \end{array}$

c) $\begin{array}{r} 6542 \\ \times\ 17 \\ \hline \end{array}$

d) $\begin{array}{r} 8564 \\ \times\ 26 \\ \hline \end{array}$

e) $\begin{array}{r} 9856 \\ \times\ 52 \\ \hline \end{array}$

f) $\begin{array}{r} 2653 \\ \times\ 52 \\ \hline \end{array}$

g) $\begin{array}{r} 7516 \\ \times\ 84 \\ \hline \end{array}$

h) $\begin{array}{r} 5095 \\ \times\ 71 \\ \hline \end{array}$

i) $\begin{array}{r} 7512 \\ \times\ 66 \\ \hline \end{array}$

j) $\begin{array}{r} 8506 \\ \times\ 37 \\ \hline \end{array}$

3 Answer these problems.

a) A cinema has 23 rows of seats with 42 seats in each row.
How many seats are there in total?

b) Charlie pays $85 each month into a savings account.
How much will he have saved in three years?

c) There are 132 pages in a maths book with 36 questions on each page.
How many questions are there in total?

d) A bus company has 47 buses. Each bus can hold 52 passengers.
What is the maximum number of people that the bus company
could take?

e) A chocolate bar weighs 386 g.
How much would a box of 18 bars of chocolate weigh,
including the box which weighs 245 g?

f) A ticket for a flight from Moscow to London costs $487.
What is the total cost of tickets for a group of 28 travellers?

g) Each side of a square tile is 76 cm.
What is the area of the tile?

h) A block of offices has 42 windows that need replacing.
Each window costs $293.
How much will it cost to have the windows replaced?

Try this

What do you notice about the numbers that make up this pair of multiplication calculations?

$$63 \times 24$$
$$36 \times 42$$

a) Work out the answer for each calculation.

b) What do you notice?

Can you find other pairs of 2-digit multiplications that do the same thing?

Multiplying by a three-digit number

Example

865×423

Estimate:
$\approx 900 \times 400$
$= 360\,000$

865×423
$= (865 \times 400) + (865 \times 20) + (865 \times 3)$
$= 346\,000 + 17\,300 + 2595$
$= 365\,895$

leading to

$$
\begin{array}{r}
865 \\
\times 423 \\
\hline
346\,000 \\
17\,300 \\
2595 \\
\hline
365\,895
\end{array}
$$

(865×400)
(865×20)
(865×3)

1 For each of the following calculations, estimate the answer then work it out.
When you have worked out the answer, check it against your estimate.

a) $\begin{array}{r} 6\ 8\ 9 \\ \times 3\ 5\ 6 \\ \hline \end{array}$

b) $\begin{array}{r} 4\ 4\ 5 \\ \times 1\ 0\ 5 \\ \hline \end{array}$

c) $\begin{array}{r} 8\ 6\ 5 \\ \times 1\ 2\ 6 \\ \hline \end{array}$

d) $\begin{array}{r} 8\ 4\ 6 \\ \times 2\ 2\ 2 \\ \hline \end{array}$

e) $\begin{array}{r} 1\ 6\ 5 \\ \times 8\ 7\ 4 \\ \hline \end{array}$

f) $\begin{array}{r} 3\ 0\ 5 \\ \times 3\ 5\ 6 \\ \hline \end{array}$

g) $\begin{array}{r} 4\ 8\ 6 \\ \times 5\ 2\ 3 \\ \hline \end{array}$

h) $\begin{array}{r} 4\ 4\ 5 \\ \times 7\ 4\ 5 \\ \hline \end{array}$

i) $\begin{array}{r} 1\ 0\ 9 \\ \times 2\ 2\ 9 \\ \hline \end{array}$

j) $\begin{array}{r} 6\ 1\ 3 \\ \times 4\ 5\ 6 \\ \hline \end{array}$

2 Answer these.

a) Small cans of lemonade contain 330 ml. If there are twenty-four cans in a layer and eight layers in a box, how much lemonade does a box contain?

b) Charlie and his family are planting a field of corn. They plant 145 seeds in each row and plant 263 rows. How many seeds do they plant altogether?

c) A factory has 274 people working in it. If they are each paid $457 a month, how much money is needed to pay all their wages each month?

d) A factory can produce 350 pencils every 5 minutes.
How many pencils can it produce in 6 days if it works 8 hours each day?

e) People on cruise ships use 260 litres of water per person per day. How much water will be used each day during a two-week cruise if a ship has 945 people on board?

f) A garage sells 890 litres of petrol on average each day. How much petrol does it sell in a year if it is open six days a week, and for forty-eight weeks of the year?

Look at the grid. It shows another method of working out the answer to the example on the previous page.

×	800	60	5	
400	320 000	24 000	2000	346 000
20	16 000	1200	100	17 300
3	2400	180	15	+ 2595
				365 895

3 Answer these, using the grid method or normal written method.

a) 115×863 b) 223×506 c) 750×470

d) 783×532 e) 447×774 f) 443×523

g) 332×774 h) 457×321 i) 772×531

j) 532×411 k) 542×222 l) 987×999

4 Use the grid method to work out the missing digits.

a) $20\boxed{} \times 419 = 85\,895$ b) $835 \times 27\boxed{} = 230\,460$ c) $436 \times 5\boxed{}7 = 255\,932$

Try this

Light travels 299 792 km each second.

a) It takes the light of the Sun 8 minutes and 19 seconds to reach Earth. How far is Earth from the Sun?

b) Light from the Sun takes 3 minutes and 13 seconds to reach Mercury, its nearest planet. How far is Mercury from the Sun?

c) The Sun's light takes 6 minutes and 1 second to reach Venus, its second planet. How far is Venus from the Sun?

Multiplying decimals

Remember... There are two ways to work out the product when multiplying decimals.

Method 1
Split the decimal fraction into the whole number and the decimal, and multiply each part separately. Then add the two numbers together.

Method 2
The number of decimal places in the product is the same as the number of decimal places in the numbers multiplied. So, multiply as with whole numbers, count the decimal places and adjust the answer.

Example 1
64.55×7

Estimate:
$\approx 65 \times 7$
$= 455$

Method 1
$(64 \times 7) + (0.55 \times 7)$
$= 448 + 3.85$
$= 451.85$

Method 2
6455×7
$= 45\,185$
64.55×7
$= 451.85$

Example 2
37.48×49

Estimate:
$\approx 37 \times 50$
$= 1850$

Method 1
$(37 \times 49) + (0.48 \times 49)$
$= 1813 + 23.52$
$= 1836.52$

Method 2

$$
\begin{array}{r}
3748 \\
\times \quad 49 \\
\hline
149\,920 \quad (3748 \times 40) \\
33\,732 \quad (3748 \times\ \ 9) \\
\hline
183\,652
\end{array}
$$

$37.48 \times 49 = 1836.52$

For each of the following calculations, estimate the answer then work it out. When you have worked out the answer, check it against your estimate.

1
a) 3.85×8
b) 4.09×7
c) 5.97×3
d) 8.67×5
e) 6.35×9
f) 8.67×7

2
a) 5.37×63
b) 2.77×25
c) 8.08×69
d) 1.57×41
e) 3.08×36
f) 7.32×74

3
a) 67.57×8
b) 32.94×9
c) 41.06×5
d) 52.32×5
e) 74.28×6
f) 26.62×7

4
a) 64.56×55
b) 13.97×43
c) 52.25×19
d) 84.26×79
e) 25.49×82
f) 90.57×44

5 Answer these.

a) Harry has bought a crate of lemonade.
It contains 16 bottles and each bottle holds 1.75 litres.
How much lemonade has he bought in total?

b) Ella is making six curtains. Each curtain needs 4.7 m of material.
How much material does she need to buy in total?

c) A lorry is carrying 47 crates of lemons. Each crate weighs 15.47 kg.
What is the total weight of the crates?

d) Beth is making 17 cakes to sell.
Each cake needs 0.45 kg of flour and 0.27 kg of sugar.
How much flour and sugar does she need?

e) A truck is carrying 1440 bricks.
If each brick weighs 1.47 kg, what weight of bricks is the truck carrying?

f) Each step that Oliver takes is 0.38 m long.
It takes him 3820 steps to walk from school to home.
How far is this?

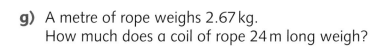

g) A metre of rope weighs 2.67 kg.
How much does a coil of rope 24 m long weigh?

h) A bottle holds 1.75 litres of shampoo.
The bottles are packed in boxes of 48.
How many millilitres of shampoo will there be in a box?

Try this

Answer this problem.

A group of 18 people book a trip to a museum.
It costs $6.45 for each adult and $3.50 for each child. The 18 people pay a total of $92.50.
How many children are in the group?

Multiplying decimals by decimals

Remember... There are two ways to work out the product when multiplying decimals.

Method 1
Split the decimal fraction into the whole number and the decimal, and multiply each part separately.

Method 2
The number of decimal places in the product is the same as the number of decimal places in the numbers multiplied. So, multiply as with whole numbers, count the decimal places and adjust the answer.

Example
7.5×8.4

Estimate:
$\approx 8 \times 8$
$= 64$

Method 1
$(7 \times 8) + (7 \times 0.4) + (0.5 \times 8) + (0.5 \times 0.4)$
$= 56 + 2.8 + 4 + 0.2$
$= 63$

Method 2

```
        75
  ×     84
      6000    (75 × 80)
       300    (75 ×  4)
      6300
```

$7.5 \times 8.4 \quad = 63$

1 For each of the following calculations, estimate the answer then work it out. When you have worked out the answer, check it against your estimate.

a) 7.8×5.3

b) 4.9×5.1

c) 8.9×8.7

d) 5.7×4.4

e) 9.3×2.8

f) 5.6×7.4

g) 4.4×6.7

h) 6.7×7.5

i) 2.8×6.2

j) 3.8×8.5

k) 7.3×9.8

l) 8.2×3.9

2 Choose pairs of numbers from this set to make the following products.

 10.8

9.6

12.7

14.3

13.8

a) 154.44

b) 121.92

c) 132.48

d) 137.16

Look at the grid. It shows another method of working out the answer to the example above.

×	7	0.5	
8	56	4	60
0.4	2.8	0.2	+ 3
			63

3 Use the grid method to answer these.

a) 4.5×3.4 b) 5.9×3.5 c) 4.7×3.7

d) 8.7×1.5 e) 2.3×7.9 f) 8.3×8.6

g) 5.6×6.4 h) 1.7×6.1 i) 9.8×5.6

j) 2.8×3.8 k) 7.3×9.2 l) 4.9×2.8

Try this

Calculate the area of each of these rectangles.

a)
7.8 cm
3.9 cm

b)
11.9 cm
4.7 cm

c)
6.6 cm
15.8 cm

d)
19.8 cm
7.4 cm

e)
12.3 cm
9.5 cm

Multiplying fractions

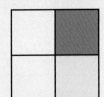

$\frac{1}{2}$ of $\frac{1}{2}$ is $\frac{1}{4}$ → This is the same as $\frac{1}{2} \times \frac{1}{2} = \frac{1}{4}$

To multiply fractions, multiply the numerators together and the denominators together. Sometimes you can cancel down the numbers to make it easier.

Example 1

$\frac{1}{2} \times \frac{1}{2}$ $\frac{1 \times 1}{2 \times 2}$ → $\frac{1}{4}$

Example 2

$\frac{2}{9} \times \frac{3}{8}$ $\frac{{}^1 2 \times {}^1 3}{{}^3 9 \times {}^4 8}$ → $\frac{1}{12}$

1 Write the answers to these multiplications. Cancel down if needed. Simplify each answer if possible.

a) $\frac{1 \times 1}{3 \times 4}$ → $\frac{\square}{\square}$

b) $\frac{3 \times 1}{4 \times 2}$ → $\frac{\square}{\square}$

c) $\frac{4 \times 2}{5 \times 3}$ → $\frac{\square}{\square}$

d) $\frac{3 \times 3}{5 \times 5}$ → $\frac{\square}{\square}$

e) $\frac{3 \times 2}{4 \times 3}$ → $\frac{\square}{\square}$

f) $\frac{1 \times 6}{3 \times 7}$ → $\frac{\square}{\square}$

g) $\frac{1 \times 8}{2 \times 10}$ → $\frac{\square}{\square}$

h) $\frac{5 \times 3}{12 \times 10}$ → $\frac{\square}{\square}$

2 Write the answers for each of these. Write each fraction in its simplest form.

a) $\frac{1}{2}$ multiplied by $\frac{4}{5}$.

b) What is a quarter multiplied by three-quarters?

c) What is $\frac{5}{9}$ multiplied by $\frac{6}{15}$?

d) Multiply $\frac{7}{9}$ by $\frac{6}{14}$.

3 Answer these. Remember to change the mixed numbers to improper fractions to work them out.

a) $3\frac{5}{7} \times 2\frac{1}{3}$ **b)** $4\frac{2}{5} \times 7\frac{3}{8}$ **c)** $4\frac{7}{9} \times 1\frac{2}{5}$ **d)** $6\frac{9}{10} \times 3\frac{4}{7}$

e) $5\frac{4}{9} \times 3\frac{1}{2}$ **f)** $8\frac{2}{3} \times 3\frac{1}{9}$ **g)** $2\frac{7}{9} \times 4\frac{3}{4}$ **h)** $5\frac{5}{7} \times 8\frac{3}{10}$

Try this

Copy and complete these.

a) $\frac{3}{4} \times \frac{1}{5} \times \frac{2}{7} =$ **b)** $\frac{5}{6} \times \frac{1}{4} \times \frac{3}{8} =$

c) $\frac{2}{9} \times \frac{3}{7} \times \frac{1}{6} =$ **d)** $\frac{5}{9} \times \frac{7}{8} \times \frac{4}{13} =$

Assessment

1 Answer these.
   a) What number is 95 times greater than 350?
   b) A box of cereal weighs 586 g. What would be the total weight of 27 boxes?
   c) A football shirt costs $27.50. The team manager orders 15 shirts.
   What is the total cost of the order?

2 Write the decimals or fractions that will come out of these function machines.

a) 0.9

b) 3.8

In → ×7.4 → Out

c) 2.7

d) 4.6

e) $\frac{1}{2}$

f) $\frac{3}{4}$

In → ×$\frac{2}{5}$ → Out

g) $\frac{5}{6}$

h) $\frac{8}{14}$

Unit 7 Division

Dividing by a single-digit number

Example

What is 48 219 divided by 6?

Estimate: 48 000 ÷ 6 = 8000

Long method	Short method
$$\begin{array}{r} 8\ 0\ 3\ 6\ \text{r}\ 3 \\ 6\overline{)4\ 8\ 2\ 1\ 9} \\ -\ 4\ 8\ 0\ 0\ 0 \\ \hline 2\ 1\ 9 \\ 1\ 8\ 0 \\ \hline 3\ 9 \\ 3\ 6 \\ \hline 3 \end{array}$$ (800×6) (30×6) (6×6)	$$\begin{array}{r} 8\ 0\ 3\ 6\ \text{r}\ 3 \\ 6\overline{)4_4 8\ 2_2 1_3 9} \end{array}$$

1 Copy and complete using the long or short method.

a) $6\overline{)3\ 1\ 9\ 5}$

b) $9\overline{)8\ 4\ 6\ 1}$

c) $4\overline{)9\ 9\ 4\ 5}$

d) $7\overline{)5\ 0\ 6\ 7}$

e) $6\overline{)1\ 1\ 9\ 6}$

f) $5\overline{)3\ 4\ 0\ 8}$

g) $3\overline{)9\ 2\ 1\ 1\ 8}$

h) $8\overline{)6\ 0\ 3\ 1\ 2}$

i) $6\overline{)4\ 9\ 0\ 8\ 1}$

j) $5\overline{)1\ 7\ 9\ 3\ 2}$

k) $7\overline{)8\ 2\ 0\ 3\ 3}$

l) $9\overline{)5\ 0\ 0\ 9\ 8}$

2 Copy and complete using the long or short method.

a) 18 474 ÷ 7

b) 19 933 ÷ 2

c) 10 938 ÷ 8

d) 45 507 ÷ 5

e) 10 384 ÷ 6

f) 21 959 ÷ 3

g) 103 516 ÷ 7

h) 478 235 ÷ 9

i) 602 175 ÷ 4

j) 587 301 ÷ 6

k) 692 136 ÷ 8

l) 509 433 ÷ 5

3 Answer these.

a) A lorry travelled a total of 1545 km in 5 days. The driver travelled the same distance each day. How far did he drive each day?

b) Three brothers have a market stall. It made $8829 profit in one month and they shared the profit equally. How much did each brother get?

c) A factory made 43 750 individual sandals in a year. How many pairs of sandals were made?

d) 10 540 kg of mangoes are packed into 5 kg boxes. How many boxes will there be?

e) 78 576 litres of milk is poured into bottles that hold 4 litres each.
How many bottles of milk will be filled?

Try this

Match each division to a remainder.

	Remainder	
	1	
38 471 ÷ 9	2	30 591 ÷ 8
	3	
44 036 ÷ 6	4	91 287 ÷ 6
	5	
21 070 ÷ 8	6	57 338 ÷ 9
	7	
97 641 ÷ 5	8	10 489 ÷ 10
	9	

Write a division for the spare remainder. ☐ ÷ ☐

Dividing by a two-digit number

Example

6812 ÷ 78

Estimate:
≈ 6400 ÷ 80
= 80

```
   7 8 )6 8 1 2
     - 6 2 4 0      (80 × 78)
       5 7 2
       5 4 6        (7 × 78)
         2 6
```

leading to

```
            8 7  r 2 6
   7 8 )6 8 1 2
     - 6 2 4 0
       5 7 2
       5 4 6
         2 6
```

6812 ÷ 78 = 87 r 26

For each of the following calculations, estimate the answer then work it out.
When you have worked out the answer, check it against your estimate.

1
a) 168 ÷ 35
b) 567 ÷ 56
c) 861 ÷ 87
d) 686 ÷ 58
e) 864 ÷ 39
f) 782 ÷ 46

2
a) 5328 ÷ 25
b) 1426 ÷ 74
c) 6712 ÷ 67
d) 6235 ÷ 64
e) 8426 ÷ 23
f) 9706 ÷ 53

3
a) 17 556 ÷ 83
b) 25 367 ÷ 52
c) 74 625 ÷ 88
d) 32 607 ÷ 63
e) 56 008 ÷ 92
f) 68 661 ÷ 44

4 Answer these.

a) Divide 4892 by 45.

b) What is 30 482 divided by 28?

c) What is the remainder when 30 075 is divided by 16?

d) How many times will 27 go into 40 245 and what is the remainder?

e) What is the remainder when 84 071 is shared between 38?

f) How many times does 56 divide into 18 355 and what is the remainder?

5 Is this statement true or false?

When you reverse the digits of any 2-digit number to make a new number and find the total of the two numbers, your answer is always divisible by 11.

Example

$34 + 43 = 77$ ➜ divisible by 11

What happens if you use pairs of 3-digit, 4-digit or 5-digit numbers?
What do you notice?

6 Answer these.

a) A factory made 4664 football shirts. A team set has 11 shirts.
   How many complete team sets were made?

b) 3402 football fans hire buses to travel to an away match. Each bus holds 54 passengers.
   How many buses will be needed to take all the fans?

c) Egg trays hold 36 eggs each.
   How many trays will be needed for 2700 eggs?

d) A man saved the same amount each month for a year to buy a car.
   The car cost $20208, so how much did he need to save each month?

e) Cloth is cut into 95 cm lengths to make scarves.
   How many scarves can be made from a roll of cloth 49 780 cm long?

f) Dates are packed into trays that hold 18 dates and one plastic fork.
   How many plastic forks will be needed for 15 732 dates?

Try this

Use each of the digits 4, 5, 6, 7, 8 and 9 once.

☐☐) ☐☐☐☐

5   6   4

9   7   8

Try to make an answer with the smallest remainder that you can.

Dividing decimals

When you divide decimals by whole numbers, use the same method as dividing with whole numbers. With short division, put a decimal point in the answer directly above the decimal point of the dividend.

Estimate the answer first so you can check if it is close.

Example

$125.26 \div 5$

Estimate:
$\approx 125 \div 5$
$= 25$

```
    _____
5 ) 1 2 5 . 2 6
  − 1 0 0            (20 × 5)
  −   2 5
        2 5          (5 × 5)
        0 . 2 6
  −     0 . 2 5      (0.05 × 5)
        0 . 0 1
  −     0 . 0 1      (0.002 × 5)
              0
```

leading to

```
        2 5 . 0 5 2
5 ) 1 2 5 . 2 6
  − 1 0
  −   2 5
        2 5
        0 . 2 6
  −     0 . 2 5
        0 . 0 1
  −     0 . 0 1
              0
```

$125.26 \div 5 = 25.052$

For each of the following calculations, estimate the answer then work it out.
When you have worked out the answer, check it against your estimate.

1
a) $64.2 \div 6$ **b)** $58.8 \div 7$ **c)** $84.1 \div 5$ **d)** $72.2 \div 4$

e) $96.4 \div 8$ **f)** $340.2 \div 7$ **g)** $464.8 \div 4$ **h)** $707.4 \div 3$

i) $765.1 \div 7$ **j)** $323.1 \div 9$

2
a) $1266.6 \div 6$ **b)** $1224.5 \div 5$ **c)** $2844.9 \div 9$ **d)** $1224.9 \div 3$

e) $1412.6 \div 4$ **f)** $65.78 \div 4$ **g)** $52.17 \div 3$ **h)** $84.23 \div 5$

i) $91.91 \div 7$ **j)** $70.26 \div 6$

3
a) $818.4 \div 66$ **b)** $670.8 \div 43$ **c)** $388.8 \div 54$ **d)** $726.3 \div 27$

e) $482.6 \div 38$ **f)** $7241.2 \div 43$ **g)** $5249.6 \div 68$ **h)** $8421.7 \div 53$

i) $8572.9 \div 37$ **j)** $4968.6 \div 26$

4 Answer these.

a) A 58.5 litre tank of water exactly fills 9 identical buckets.
 What is the capacity of each bucket?

b) Six dining chairs cost $151.50.
 What is the price of one chair?

c) A path is 23.36 m long and is made with 16 square paving slabs.
 What is the length of each paving slab?

d) Lucy travels 477.3 km in her car and uses 37 l of petrol.
 How many kilometres does her car travel on a litre of petrol on average?

e) A lorry is carrying 24 identical washing machines. The total weight of the load is 1898.4 kg.
 How much does each washing machine weigh?

f) An apartment block is 113.9 m high. It has 34 floors in it.
 How high is each floor?

g) Mike buys 68 bricks. They weigh 144.84 kg in total.
 How much does one brick weigh?

h) The total rent on a house for a year is $882.48.
 What is the cost each month?

Try this

Divide a number from the ring by a number from the box so that the quotient is one of the numbers below.

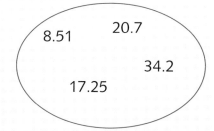

8.51   20.7   34.2   17.25

2.3   3.6

a) 7.5   **b)** 9.5   **c)** 3.7   **d)** 5.75

Remainders as decimals

Sometimes you need to have a decimal answer to a division problem, not a remainder as a whole number.

Example 1

What is 4751 divided by 4?

Estimate: 4800 ÷ 4 = 1200

Extra zeros are needed to complete the division with a quotient written as a decimal number. Zeros after the decimal point do not change the value of the number.

$$\begin{array}{r} 1\ 1\ 8\ 7\ .\ 7\ 5 \\ 4\overline{)4\ 7\ {}^35\ {}^31\ .\ {}^30\ {}^20} \end{array}$$

So 4751 ÷ 4 = 1187.75

Some divisions with decimal answers go on and on … These are called recurring decimals.

Example 2

52 ÷ 7

$$\begin{array}{r} 7\ .\ 4\ 2\ 8\ 5\ldots \\ 7\overline{)5\ 2\ .\ {}^30\ {}^20\ {}^60\ {}^40} \end{array}$$

With divisions like this, round the decimal answers to one decimal place (7.4) or two decimal places (7.43).

---

1 Write approximate answers, then calculate the exact answer.

a) 7283 ÷ 5 ➜ estimate = ☐

actual answer = ☐

b) 9437 ÷ 8 ➜ estimate = ☐

actual answer = ☐

c) 3906 ÷ 4 ➜ estimate = ☐

actual answer = ☐

d) 4177 ÷ 2 ➜ estimate = ☐

actual answer = ☐

e) 9363 ÷ 4 ➜ estimate = ☐

actual answer = ☐

f) 4194 ÷ 8 ➜ estimate = ☐

actual answer = ☐

2 Answer these. Work out the quotient to two decimal places.

a) $9\overline{)2742.7}$ **b)** $5\overline{)3819.7}$ **c)** $8\overline{)7323.5}$ **d)** $7\overline{)1984.9}$

e) $3\overline{)7418.92}$ **f)** $6\overline{)3918.53}$ **g)** $9\overline{)2119.61}$ **h)** $8\overline{)4737.63}$

3 This table shows the amount of money saved by six people. Each month they save the same amount. Copy and complete the table, calculating the amount saved each month.

Name	Amount saved each month	Number of months	Total saved
Joe		5	$4721
Jack		4	$6225
Anna		10	$3097
Oliver		8	$5426
Emily		4	$3915
Lily		5	$7438

4 Answer these.

a) This piece of wood is divided into 4 equal lengths. How long is each length?

173 cm

b) A group of five people share out $2342 between them. How much do they each get?

c) A water tank holds 182 litres. It is emptied and exactly fills 8 large containers. What is the capacity of each container?

d) James saves the same amount each week. After 12 weeks he has saved $81. How much does he save each week?

e) A lorry holds 1293 kg of grain. It is divided equally into 5 containers. How much grain is in each container?

Try this

Work out the quotient for each of these to two decimal places.

a) $6.25 \div 0.7 = \square$ **b)** $4.01 \div 0.6 = \square$ **c)** $9.06 \div 0.9 = \square$

d) $12.63 \div 0.8 = \square$ **e)** $24.75 \div 0.5 = \square$ **f)** $31.43 \div 0.3 = \square$

Dividing fractions

When dividing fractions, we turn the **divisor** upside down and multiply.

Example 1

$$\frac{3}{5} \div \frac{3}{10}$$

$$\rightarrow \quad \frac{3}{5} \times \frac{10}{3}$$

$$\rightarrow \quad \frac{{}^1\cancel{3} \times {}^2\cancel{10}}{{}^1\cancel{5} \times {}^1\cancel{3}} \rightarrow \frac{2}{1} = 2$$

Example 2

What is $\frac{7}{8}$ divided by **4**?

$$\frac{7}{8} \div 4 = \frac{7}{8} \div \frac{4}{1}$$

$$\rightarrow \quad \frac{7 \times 1}{8 \times 4} \rightarrow \frac{7}{32}$$

1 Complete these divisions and write each answer in its simplest form. Cancel down if needed.

a) $\frac{1}{2} \div 3 \rightarrow \frac{1}{2} \div \frac{3}{1} \rightarrow \frac{1}{2} \times \frac{1}{3} \rightarrow \frac{\square}{\square}$

b) $\frac{3}{5} \div 4 \rightarrow \frac{3}{5} \div \frac{4}{1} \rightarrow \frac{3}{5} \times \frac{\square}{\square} \rightarrow \frac{\square}{\square}$

c) $\frac{2}{3} \div 6 \rightarrow \frac{2}{3} \div \frac{6}{1} \rightarrow \frac{\square}{\square} \times \frac{\square}{\square} \rightarrow \frac{\square}{\square}$

d) $\frac{4}{7} \div 8 \rightarrow \frac{\square}{\square} \div \frac{\square}{\square} \rightarrow \frac{\square}{\square} \times \frac{\square}{\square} \rightarrow \frac{\square}{\square}$

e) $\frac{1}{5} \div \frac{1}{3} \rightarrow \frac{1}{5} \times \frac{3}{1} \rightarrow \frac{\square}{\square}$

f) $\frac{2}{3} \div \frac{2}{9} \rightarrow \frac{2}{3} \times \frac{\square}{\square} \rightarrow \frac{\square}{\square}$

g) $\frac{2}{7} \div \frac{3}{4} \rightarrow \frac{\square}{\square} \times \frac{\square}{\square} \rightarrow \frac{\square}{\square}$

h) $\frac{9}{15} \div \frac{3}{10} \rightarrow \frac{\square}{\square} \times \frac{\square}{\square} \rightarrow \frac{\square}{\square}$

2 Complete these divisions and write each answer in its simplest form. Cancel down if needed.

a) $\frac{3}{5} \div \frac{1}{4} =$

b) $\frac{1}{3} \div \frac{1}{7} =$

c) $\frac{3}{4} \div \frac{3}{8} =$

d) $\frac{4}{5} \div \frac{1}{10} =$

e) $\frac{7}{12} \div \frac{1}{2} =$

f) $\frac{1}{8} \div \frac{3}{4} =$

g) $\frac{2}{5} \div \frac{7}{10} =$

h) $\frac{5}{9} \div \frac{1}{3} =$

3 Write the answers for each of these. Write each fraction in its simplest form.

a) Divide $\frac{1}{6}$ by 3.

b) What is $\frac{9}{20}$ divided by 5?

c) What is a third divided by a half?

d) What is $\frac{3}{8}$ divided by $\frac{1}{4}$?

e) Divide $\frac{2}{3}$ by $\frac{1}{5}$.

f) What is $\frac{1}{8}$ divided by $\frac{2}{3}$?

Assessment

1 Read and answer these.

a) Divide 5102 by 3. Write the answer to 2 decimal places.

b) What is 7233 divided by 14? Write the answer to 2 decimal places.

c) What is the remainder when 2941 is divided by 18?

d) How many times will 6 divide into 11.55? Write the answer to 2 decimal places.

e) What is the remainder when 40895 is divided by 23?

f) What is 7224.34 divided by 5? Write the answer to 2 decimal places.

2 Write the missing fractions in these function machines.

a) $\frac{1}{2}$

b) $\frac{7}{12}$

c) $\frac{3}{4}$

d) $\frac{8}{9}$

e) ☐

f) ☐

g) ☐

h) ☐

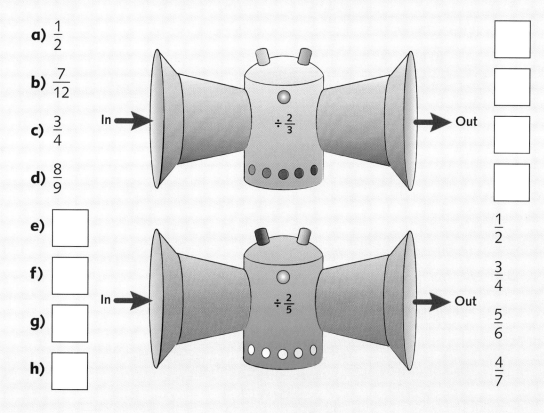

$\frac{1}{2}$

$\frac{3}{4}$

$\frac{5}{6}$

$\frac{4}{7}$

Mixed operations

1 What is $(9^2 - 28) + (4^2 \times 3)$?

   a) 101   **b)** 77   **c)** 97

2 What is $3\,987\,426 + 4\,830\,947$?

   a) 7 818 273   **b)** 8 818 373

   c) 8 808 373

3 What is $9 \times (6^2 - 8) + 19$?

   a) 423   **b)** 235   **c)** 271

4 What is the missing number?

$$\boxed{} + 3\,928\,301 = 21\,905\,491$$

   a) 25 833 792   **b)** 17 977 190

   c) 18 782 481

5 This table shows the approximate area of some of the largest deserts in the world.

Desert	Location	Area (square kilometres)
Sahara	Morocco, Western Sahara, Algeria, Tunisia, Libya, Egypt, Mauritania, Mali, Niger, Chad, Ethiopia, Eritrea, Somalia	3 510 942
Arabian	Saudi Arabia, Kuwait, Qatar, United Arab Emirates, Oman, Yemen	1 034 827
Gobi	China, Mongolia	501 209
Patagonian	Argentina	262 058
Great Victoria	Australia	251 974
Kalahari	Botswana, South Africa, Namibia	220 105

Use the table to answer these.

a) What is the difference in area between the Sahara and Gobi deserts?

b) What is the total area of the Sahara and the Arabian desert?

c) How much greater in size is the Patagonian desert than the Kalahari?

d) Which two deserts total $753\,183 \text{ km}^2$ in area?

e) True or false? The Sahara desert is greater in size than all the other five deserts put together.
Calculate the difference to prove your answer.

6 Use the digits 1, 2 and 3 to complete each calculation.

a) $(\boxed{} + \boxed{}) \times \boxed{} = 9$

b) $\boxed{} \times (\boxed{} - \boxed{}) = 4$

c) $\boxed{} - (\boxed{} \times \boxed{}) = 1$

7 Work out the missing numbers.

a) $(234 \div \boxed{}) + 7 = 20$

b) $(592 \div \boxed{}) - 18 = 56$

c) $(\boxed{} + 210) \times 9 = 3105$

d) $(7 \times \boxed{}) - 37 = 1083$

e) $(\boxed{} \div 8) + 75 = 120$

f) $(49 \times \boxed{}) + 18 = 214$

g) $(\boxed{} \div 15) - 14 = 9$

h) $(\boxed{} - 45) \times 15 = 1425$

8 Copy these statements, using <, > or = to make each one true.

a) $(8^2 \times 3^2) + (9^2 \div 3) \boxed{} (7^2 + 18) + (6^2 - 18)$

b) $3^2 + (9 \times 4^2) - 8^2 \boxed{} (5^2 \times 2) - (8^2 \div 4)$

c) $(9 \times 5) - (2^4 \div 4) + 7^2 \boxed{} 10^2 \times (216 \div 8) - 4^3$

d) $6^2 + (9^2 - 38) + (2^3 + 14) \boxed{} 4^2 \times (7^2 + 4) + (2^3 \times 3^3)$

Try this

The four missing numbers in this calculation are different and are less than 6.

$(\boxed{}^2 - \boxed{}^2) \times (\boxed{}^2 + \boxed{}^2) = \underline{\hspace{2cm}}$

Find three possible solutions.

Multiplication

1 What is $\frac{2}{9}$ multiplied by $\frac{3}{4}$?

   a) $\frac{1}{9}$ **b)** $\frac{1}{6}$ **c)** $\frac{5}{13}$

2 What is 328 multiplied by 67?

   a) 20 926   **b)** 21 976   **c)** 21 676

3 What is a one-third multiplied by three-quarters?

   a) $\frac{1}{4}$ **b)** $\frac{1}{12}$ **c)** $\frac{2}{3}$

4 $2.45 \times 1.8 = \boxed{}$

   a) 4.41   **b)** 3.3   **c)** 44.1

5 For each night of a Firework Fiesta the cost of a ticket was different.

Day	Number of tickets sold	Cost of a ticket	Approximate total	Exact total
Monday	349	$12		
Tuesday	291	$14		
Wednesday	446	$17		
Thursday	439	$21		
Friday	518	$24		

   a) What is the approximate total amount taken in ticket sales each day?

   b) Calculate the exact amount taken each day.

6 Use the digits 4, 5, 6 and 7 to complete each multiplication.

   a) $\boxed{}\boxed{}\boxed{} \times \boxed{} = 2628$

   b) $\boxed{}\boxed{}\boxed{} \times \boxed{} = 3948$

   c) $\boxed{}\boxed{}.\boxed{} \times \boxed{} = 337$

   d) $\boxed{}\boxed{}.\boxed{} \times \boxed{} = 447$

7 **a)** What is 123×45?

   b) Use the same five digits, 1, 2, 3, 4 and 5, to make these true.

      $\boxed{}\boxed{}\boxed{} \times \boxed{}\boxed{} < 1\,2\,3 \times 4\,5$

      $\boxed{}\boxed{}\boxed{} \times \boxed{}\boxed{} > 1\,2\,3 \times 4\,5$

8 Choose pairs of numbers from this set to make the following products.

| 19.7 | 13.6 | 9.4 | 17.2 | 8.7 |

a) 118.32   b) 161.68   c) 185.18   d) 267.92

9 Match each fraction calculation to the correct answer.

$$\frac{1}{2} \times \frac{1}{5} \qquad \frac{2}{7} \times \frac{1}{2} \qquad \frac{3}{4} \times \frac{4}{27} \qquad \frac{1}{2} \times \frac{2}{5}$$

$$\frac{1}{2} \qquad \frac{1}{3} \qquad \frac{1}{4} \qquad \frac{1}{5} \qquad \frac{1}{6}$$

$$\frac{1}{7} \qquad \frac{1}{8} \qquad \frac{1}{9} \qquad \frac{1}{10}$$

$$\frac{1}{3} \times \frac{1}{2} \qquad \frac{1}{2} \times \frac{1}{4} \qquad \frac{1}{2} \times \frac{1}{2} \qquad \frac{2}{3} \times \frac{1}{2} \qquad \frac{2}{3} \times \frac{3}{4}$$

10 Answer these. Remember to change the mixed numbers to improper fractions to work them out.

a) $4\frac{1}{3} \times 2\frac{1}{5}$ b) $5\frac{2}{3} \times 7\frac{5}{8}$ c) $2\frac{7}{9} \times 1\frac{2}{5}$ d) $3\frac{3}{10} \times 4\frac{5}{7}$

e) $1\frac{4}{5} \times 4\frac{1}{2}$ f) $3\frac{2}{3} \times 4\frac{1}{9}$ g) $6\frac{1}{9} \times 2\frac{3}{4}$ h) $1\frac{2}{7} \times 3\frac{7}{10}$

Try this

Answer this problem.

Sam buys some pens and pencils. The pens cost $3.45 each and the pencils are $0.80 each.
Altogether he buys 5 more pencils than pens, and he spends $21 altogether.
How many pens and pencils does he buy?

Division

1 What is the missing number?

$918 \div \boxed{} = 27$

a) 34   b) 44   c) 36

2 What is $\frac{1}{10}$ divided by 5?

a) $\frac{1}{2}$ b) $\frac{1}{50}$ c) 50

3 What is 6152 divided by 7, with the quotient to 2 decimal places?

a) 878.86   b) 878.8   c) 879.86

4 What is a three-fifths divided by three-quarters?

a) $\frac{9}{20}$ b) $\frac{2}{3}$ c) $\frac{4}{5}$

5 Each day a concert is held in a large hall. This chart shows the number of tickets sold and the number of chairs in each row. The rows of chairs are filled up one at a time.

Day	Number of tickets sold	Number of chairs in each row
Monday	426	18
Tuesday	655	25
Wednesday	512	24
Thursday	380	16
Friday	693	27

For each day:

a) How many rows are completely full?

b) How many rows are needed altogether?

c) Work out the fraction of the final row that is used.

d) Write the number of occupied rows as a mixed number.

6 a) Use whole numbers to complete this division in three different ways.

$\boxed{} \div \boxed{} = 6.4$

b) Use your answer to part (a) to write three different ways to complete each division.

$\boxed{} \div \boxed{} = 12.8$ $\boxed{} \div \boxed{} = 3.2$

7 Use the digits 4, 5, 6, 7, 8 and 9 twice each to make this statement true.

$\boxed{}\boxed{}.\boxed{} \div \boxed{} < \boxed{}\boxed{}.\boxed{} \div \boxed{} < \boxed{}\boxed{}.\boxed{} \div \boxed{}$

8 Katy is planting seeds in rows. She plants 6 beans all the same distance apart in a row 100 cm long.

There are 5 gaps between 6 beans. Each gap must be 20 cm long, because 100 ÷ 5 = 20. She still has these seeds to plant

a) 9 Lettuce seeds — in a row 54 cm long

b)  12 Tomato seeds — in a row 95 cm long

c) 16 Cucumber seeds — in a row 115 cm long

d) 13 Peas — in a row 106 cm long

For each packet find the length of each gap. Write any remainder as a decimal, rounding to the nearest hundredth.

9 Find the missing whole numbers in these divisions.

a) $70.2 ÷ \boxed{} = 23.4$

b) $157.6 ÷ \boxed{} = 19.7$

c) $214.8 ÷ \boxed{} = 35.8$

d) $491.4 ÷ \boxed{} = 54.6$

e) $52.96 ÷ \boxed{} = 13.24$

f) $333.6 ÷ \boxed{} = 41.7$

g) $178.2 ÷ \boxed{} = 29.7$

h) $187.5 ÷ \boxed{} = 37.5$

Try this

Answer these. What do you notice about the answers?

a) $\frac{1}{3} × \frac{1}{4} =$ 　　　　$\frac{1}{3} ÷ \frac{1}{4} =$

$\frac{1}{4} × \frac{1}{3} =$ 　　　　$\frac{1}{4} ÷ \frac{1}{3} =$

b) $\frac{1}{4} × 2 =$ 　　　　$\frac{1}{4} ÷ 2 =$

$2 × \frac{1}{4} =$ 　　　　$2 ÷ \frac{1}{4} =$

Lines, segments and rays: revision

Remember…
A **line** can go on for ever in both directions.

A **line segment** is a part of a line that has two end points.

This line segment is CD.
C and D are the two end points.

A **ray** is part of a line. It has one end point and the other end goes on and on for ever.

This ray is XY.

Intersecting lines always cross each other somewhere.

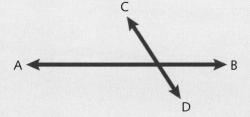

Parallel lines are the same distance apart from each other all the way along their length. Even if the lines are made longer, they will never meet.

Line AB is parallel to line CD.
Line AC is parallel to line BD.

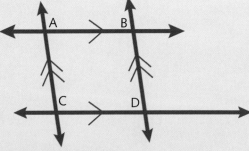

Perpendicular lines are lines that meet at a right angle.

Angles ABC and ABD are both right angles.
Line AB is perpendicular to line CD.

1 Name each of the following.
Choose from one of these.

parallel lines   **perpendicular lines**   **intersecting lines**

a)

b)

c)

d)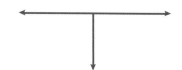

e)

f)

2 Write whether these are examples of lines, segments or rays.
Use the letters to name them.

a)

b)

c)

d)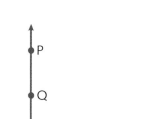

e)

f)

Try this

Look at this diagram and write the letters that show the following.

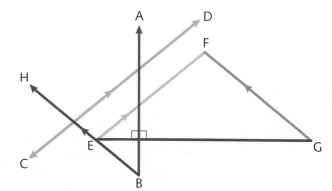

a) intersecting lines
b) rays
c) parallel lines
d) line segments

Constructing perpendicular and parallel lines

A set-square is a mathematical instrument.
It is used for measuring and drawing right angles.
It can also be used for finding or drawing perpendicular lines.

By sliding the bottom edge of a set-square along
a ruler it can also be used for finding or drawing
parallel lines.

1 Copy and complete these drawings using a ruler and set-square.

a) Draw a perpendicular line to
AB from point C.

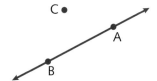

b) Draw a perpendicular line to XY from
point Z.

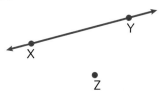

c) Draw a line CE from point E, perpendicular
to CD. Make the line CE = 4 cm.

d) Draw a line through point F,
perpendicular to GH. Label the line JK,
and make the line JK = 5 cm.

e) Draw a parallel line to AB going
through point C.

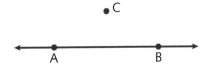

f) Draw a parallel line to XY going
through point A.

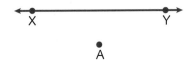

2 Use a set-square and ruler to draw parallel and perpendicular lines for these shapes.

a) Draw a square of side length 6 cm.

- Draw AB, where AB = 6 cm.
- Use a set-square to draw perpendicular and parallel lines.
- Draw the shape and measure to check accuracy.

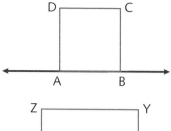

b) Draw a rectangle of side length 5 cm and 3.5 cm.

- Draw WX, where WX = 5 cm.
- Use a set-square to draw perpendicular and parallel lines.
- Draw the shape and measure to check accuracy.

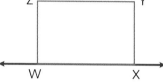

Try this

Use a set-square and ruler to draw each of the following shapes.
Use the symbols > and >> to show all the pairs of parallel lines.
Use the symbol for a right angle, ⌐, to show all the perpendicular lines.

a)

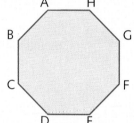

b)

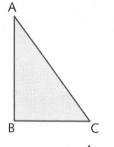

c)

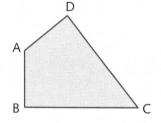

d)

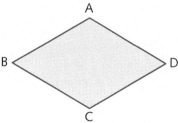

e)

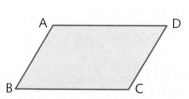

f)

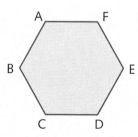

g)

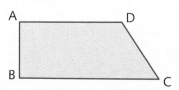

h)

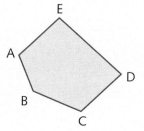

Angles

Remember...
Angles are measured in degrees (°). There are 360° in a full circle.

- Angles on a straight line add up to 180°.

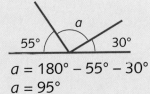

$a = 180° - 55° - 30°$
$a = 95°$

- Angles at a point add up to 360°.

$b = 360° - 140° - 135°$
$b = 85°$

- Opposite angles are equal.

$p = 120°$ $q = 60°$
$p + q = 180°$

- The angles of a triangle add up to 180°.

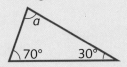

$a = 180° - 70° - 30°$
$a = 80°$

---

1 Calculate the missing angles. Do not use a protractor.

a)

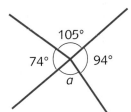

b)

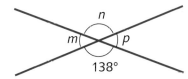

c)

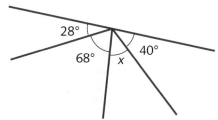

d)

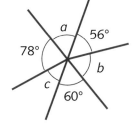

e)

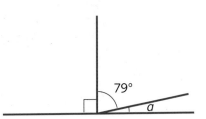

f)

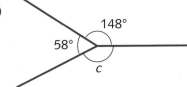

g)

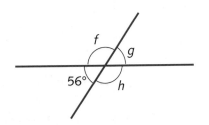

h)

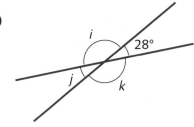

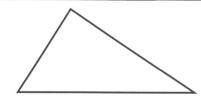

A scalene triangle has no equal angles and no equal sides.

An isosceles triangle has two equal sides and two equal angles.

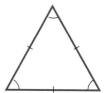

An equilateral triangle has three equal sides and three equal angles.

2 Calculate the size of the missing angles on these triangles. Do not use a protractor.

a)

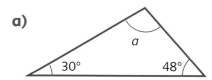

30° a 48°

b)

85° b 74°

c)

55° 46° c

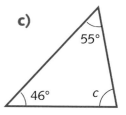

d)

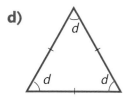

d d d

e)

38° e x

f)

32° f f

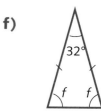

g)

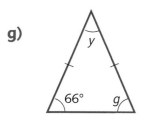

y 66° g

h)

h w 20°

i)

54° i i

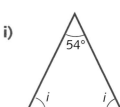

Try this

Line AB intersects parallel lines CD and EF.
Calculate each of the missing angles.

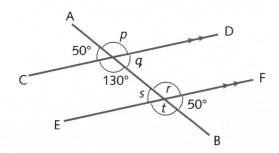

A p D 50° q 130° s r F t 50° C E B

What do you notice about the angles?

Measuring and drawing angles

We use a protractor to measure and draw angles.
A protractor has a clockwise and an anti-clockwise scale. This is so that you can measure angles to the left or right.

It is a good idea to estimate the angle first and then measure it.
- If you think the angle is an acute angle then your answer should be less than 90°.
- If you think the angle is an obtuse angle then your answer should be between 90° and 180°.
- If you think the angle is a reflex angle then your answer should be greater than 180°.

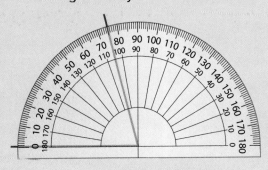

To draw an angle of 98°:

Draw a single base line.

Line up the protractor so that the centre is at one end, whichever one you wish to be the vertex of the angle.

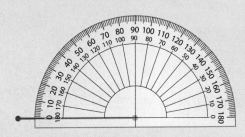

Mark off the angle.

Draw a line to show 98°.

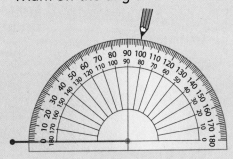

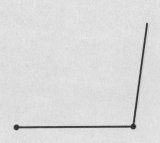

1 Draw and label each of the following angles.
a)	43°	**b)**	147°	**c)**	68°	**d)**	52°
e)	91°	**f)**	161°	**g)**	83°	**h)**	8°
i)	170°	**j)**	114°	**k)**	172°	**l)**	39°

2 Look at each of these angles. Decide what type of angle each one is: acute angle, obtuse angle or reflex angle and write it down. Then use a protractor to measure each angle.

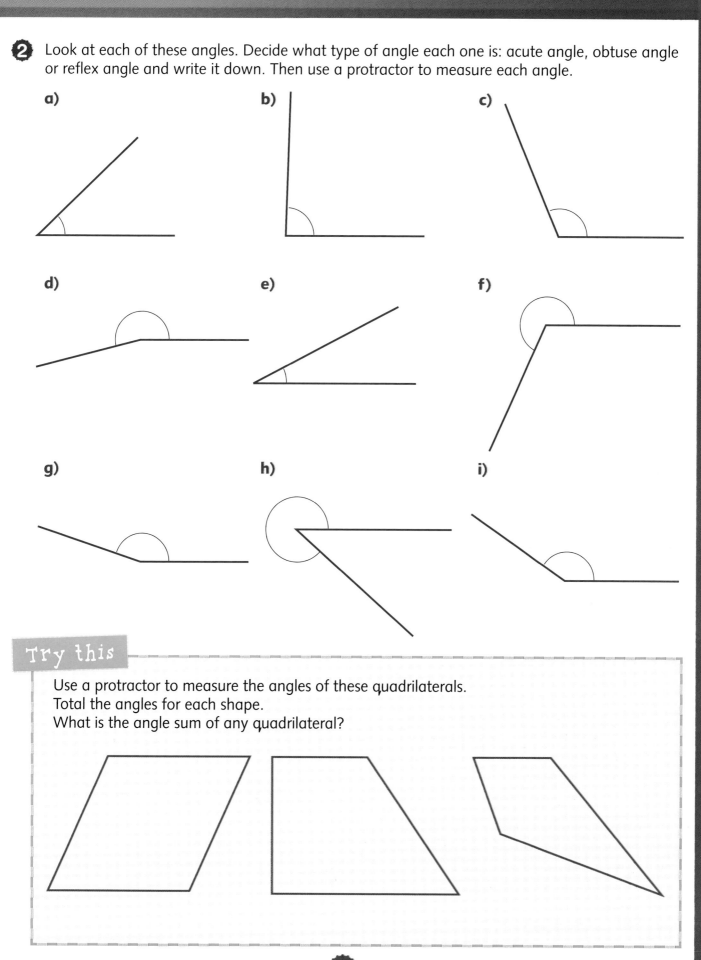

a)

b)

c)

d)

e)

f)

g)

h)

i)

Try this

Use a protractor to measure the angles of these quadrilaterals.
Total the angles for each shape.
What is the angle sum of any quadrilateral?

Constructing triangles

You can draw an accurate triangle with this information:

- the length of two sides and the angle between them

- the length of one side and the angles at either end.

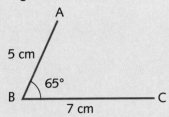

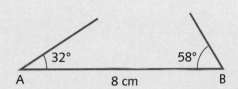

1 Use a ruler and protractor to copy and complete these triangles.
The lengths and angles of these diagrams are not exact.

a)

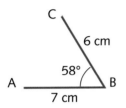

b)

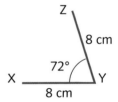

c)

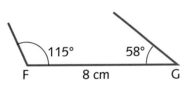

d)

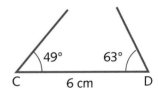

2 Measure and record each of the angles and lengths of sides for the triangles you have drawn.

3 Use a pair of compasses to draw a triangle with sides of 60 mm, 45 mm and 55 mm.

Follow these instructions:

Step 1
Draw a line 60 mm long.

Step 2
Set your compasses at 45 mm and, with the compass point on A, draw an arc.

Step 3
Set your compasses at 55 mm.
With the compass point on B, draw another arc, to intersect the first at C.

Step 4
Use a ruler to join AC and BC.

1

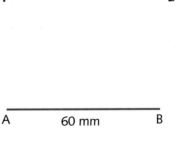

2

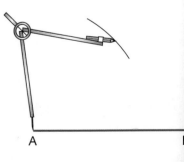

3

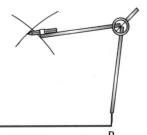

4

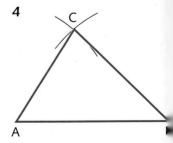

4 Use compasses and a ruler to draw these triangles.

	Side 1	Side 2	Side 3
a	40 mm	60 mm	80 mm
b	45 mm	45 mm	65 mm
c	42 mm	56 mm	69 mm
d	52 mm	52 mm	52 mm

Try this

Measure and record the angles of your four triangles above.
a) What sort of triangles have you drawn?
b) Is the largest angle always opposite the longest side?

Assessment

These are sketches of some triangles.

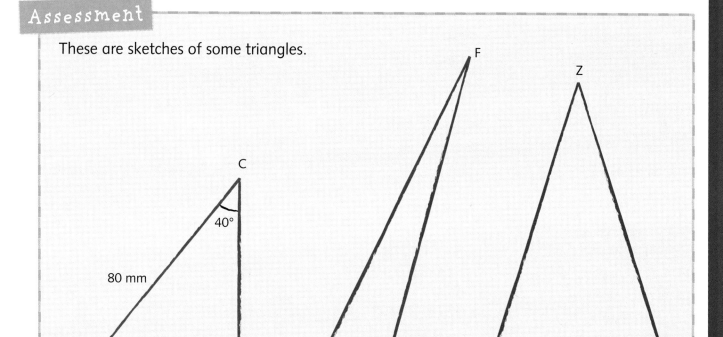

1 Draw the triangles accurately on paper.
2 Measure and label the missing angles.
3 What is the angle total for each triangle?

85

Polygons

A polygon is any 2-D shape with straight sides.
The sides and angles of a regular polygon are all equal.

regular pentagon   irregular pentagon

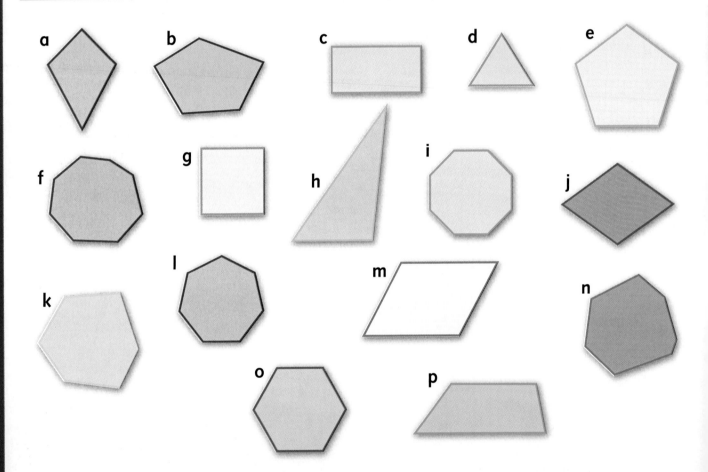

1   Look at the shapes above. Copy and complete the table.

Shape	Number of sides	Number of angles	Number of lines of symmetry	Number of pairs of parallel sides	Regular or irregular	Name of shape
a.						
b.						
c.						

2 Copy and complete this table.
Research information about each shape and only put a tick if it is true for all shapes of that type.

	quadrilateral	parallelogram	rhombus	rectangle	square	kite	trapezium
4 sides	✓						
All sides same length					✓		
Opposite sides same length		✓					
Adjacent sides same length							
Both pairs of opposite sides parallel							
A pair of opposite sides parallel							
At least 1 right angle							
4 right angles							

Try this

Say whether each of these statements is **always**, **sometimes** or **never** true.
Use the table above to help you.

a) Rectangles are parallelograms

b) Rhombuses are parallelograms

c) Rhombuses are squares

d) Squares are rectangles

e) Trapeziums are parallelograms

f) Rectangles are squares

g) Kites are parallelograms

h) Squares are rhombuses

Congruence and tessellations

When shapes are identical we say they are congruent.
Congruent shapes can be reflections of each other.
These shapes are congruent.

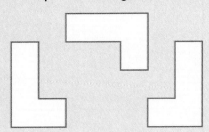

A tessellation is a tiling pattern made by repeating a congruent shape over and over again.

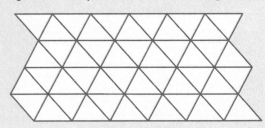

1 For each of these, write down the shape that is not congruent to the others.

a)

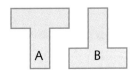

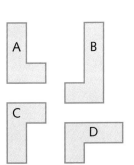

b)

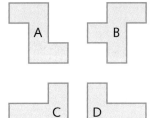

c)

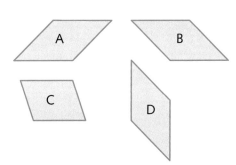

d)

2 Copy these quadrilaterals and name each one.

a) Join one diagonal on each shape to give two triangles.
   Which shapes have two congruent triangles?

b) Join the other diagonal on each shape to give four triangles.
   Which shapes have four congruent triangles?

3 Use squared paper to draw these tessellations.

a) All quadrilaterals tessellate.
Copy one of these or make up your own tessellation with any congruent quadrilateral.

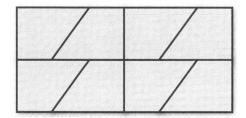
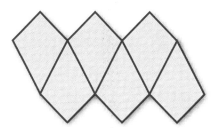

b) All triangles tessellate.
Draw a tessellation of triangles.

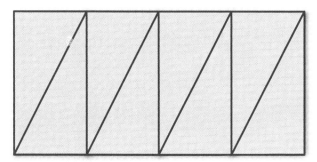

c) Many other shapes tessellate.
Experiment with some shapes of your own

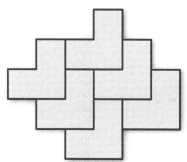

Try this

Make shape tiles in the following way to make a tessellated pattern.

a) Start with a square of card.
Cut out a shape.

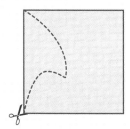

b) Slide the cut-out piece to the other side of the shape and stick it on with tape.

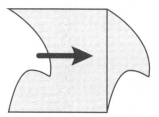

c) Draw round your shape tile on to paper to make a tessellated pattern.

You can start from other shapes such as these.

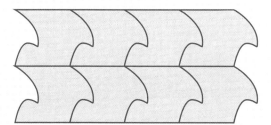
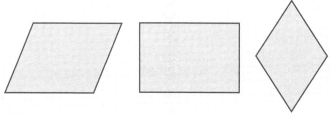

Enlarging shapes

Geometrical shapes are said to be **similar** if they are the *same* in shape but *different* in size. One shape is an enlargement of another.

 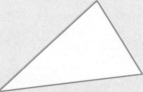

1 Follow these instructions to find a way of enlarging shapes and pictures.

a) Draw a triangle. Draw a dot about 3 cm to one side of the triangle.

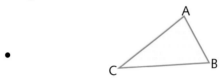

b) Draw straight lines from the dot to go through each corner of the triangle.

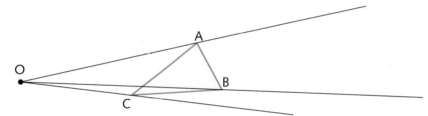

c) Measure and put marks so that:
AE = OA
BF = OB
CG = OC

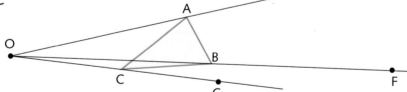

d) Join EFG.

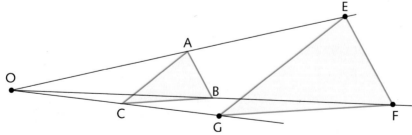

2 Measure the angles of the two triangles.
What do you notice?

3 Enlarge more triangles in the same way. What happens if you make:
AE = 2 × OA,   BF = 2 × OB   and   CG = 2 × OC?

4 Draw some of your own shapes and then enlarge them.

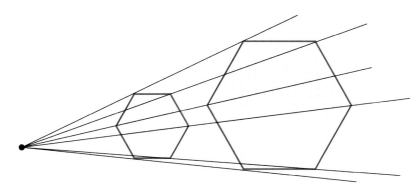

Try this

Follow these instructions to make an instrument that enlarges drawings.

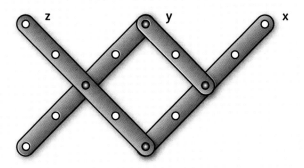

a) Cut out four strips of strong card, or use plastic geostrips.
Three of them are 12 cm in length and one is 6 cm.

b) Punch holes in them and use fasteners to clip them together in the four places shown.

c) Fasten point **x** to your paper with a drawing pin.

d) Put a sharpened pencil in the hole at point **z**.

e) Trace over a picture by going over it at point **y**. The picture should be drawn and enlarged at point **z**.

Try enlarging these simple pictures.

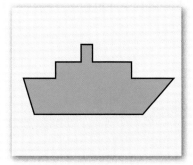

Polyhedra

Polyhedra are 3-D shapes with each face made from a polygon.

3-D shapes are made up of **faces**, **edges** and **vertices** (corners).

A cuboid has 6 faces, 12 edges and 8 vertices.

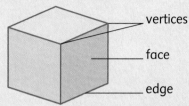

vertices

face

edge

1 Match each description to the shape name to complete the sentence.

a) A triangular prism has …   … 4 triangular faces.

b) A cube has …   … 2 hexagonal faces and 6 rectangular faces.

c) A tetrahedron has …   … 2 triangular faces and 3 rectangular faces.

d) A hexagonal prism has …   … 6 rectangular faces.

e) A square-based pyramid has …   … 6 square faces.

f) A cuboid has …   … 1 square face and 4 triangular faces.

2 Write the name for each shape.

a)

b)

c)

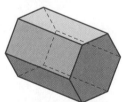

d)

e)

f)

3 Find the number of faces, edges and vertices on each shape and complete this chart.

Name of shape	Number of faces	Number of vertices	Number of edges
Tetrahedron			
Square-based pyramid			
Triangular prism			
Cuboid			
Pentagonal prism			
Hexagonal prism			

4 Look at the number of faces, edges and vertices of each shape on the chart.
Can you spot a rule or patterns between the numbers?

5 There is a formula for linking the number of faces, edges and vertices on a polyhedron:

faces + vertices – edges = 2

This called Euler's formula. For example, a cube has 6 faces, 8 vertices and 12 edges.
6 + 8 – 12 = 2

Check whether Euler's formula works for the shapes in the table above.

Try this

Here are some shapes with long names.

octahedron   dodecahedron
cuboctahedron   rhombicuboctahedron

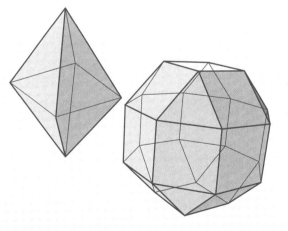
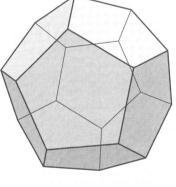
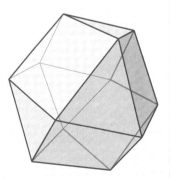

a) Carry out some research to find which shape goes with each name.
b) Describe each shape.
c) Try drawing a net of one of the shapes.

Nets and solids

The **net** of a shape is what it looks like when it is opened out flat.

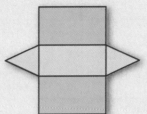

net of a triangular prism

1 Write the name of each of these shapes from its net.

a)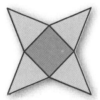

b)

c)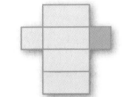

d)

e)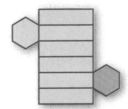

f)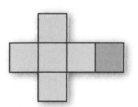

2 The rule for putting spots on the faces of dice is that opposite faces total 7.
This is the net of a dice.
How many spots would go on faces A, B and C?

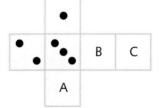

3 Which of the following are nets of cuboids?

a)

b)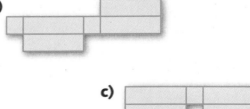

d)

c)

Two of these nets will fold up to make a tetrahedron.

Which is the odd one out?

a)

b)

c)

Assessment

This is a diagram of the net of a solid.

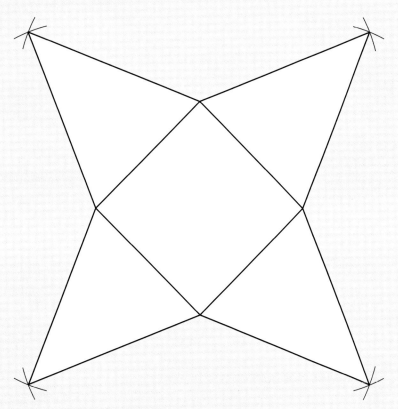

1   What is the name of the solid?
2   What types of triangles make four of the faces?
3   How many vertices does the solid have?
4   Measure the shape. Use compasses and a ruler to draw the net on plain paper.
5   Cut out the net. Fold it to make a solid.

Parts of a circle

Look at the parts of a circle.

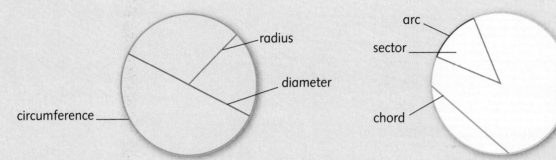

The **circumference** is the perimeter of a circle.

The **diameter** is a straight line drawn through the centre of a circle. It divides the circle into two halves.

The **radius** (plural 'radii') is the distance from the centre of the circle to its circumference. All radii of a circle are the same length.

A **sector** of a circle is like a slice of pie. The sides of the slice are radii of the circle.

A **chord** is a straight line which joins two points on the circumference.

An **arc** is any part of the circumference of a circle.

1 Use a pair of compasses, a ruler and a sharp pencil to draw a circle with a radius of:

a) 6 cm   **b)** 3 cm   **c)** 5 cm

d) 3.5 cm   **e)** 6.5 cm   **f)** 4.5 cm

2 Use a pair of compasses, a ruler and a sharp pencil to draw a circle with a diameter of:

a) 108 mm   **b)** 82 mm   **c)** 146 mm

d) 96 mm   **e)** 74 mm   **f)** 88 mm

3 Draw a circle with a radius of 8 cm.
Colour and label the following parts of your circle.

        circumference   diameter   radius   chord   arc   sector

4 These are concentric circles.

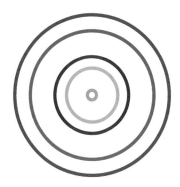

a) Draw concentric circles with radii of 3 cm, 4 cm and 5 cm.

b) Draw another set of concentric circles with the same radii. Make the centre of these circles on the circumference of the first set so that the circles overlap.

c) Colour the pattern.

Try this

1 a) Draw a circle with a radius of 30 mm.
  b) Draw a vertical diameter.
  c) Set a pair of compasses at 10 mm and mark off each 10 mm round the circumference.
  d) Put your compass point where each arc meets the circumference and draw circles that exactly touch the diameter line.

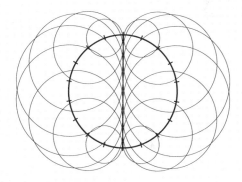

This pattern is called a nephroid.

2 a) Draw a circle with a radius of 30 mm.
  b) Draw a vertical diameter.
  c) Set a pair of compasses at 10 mm and mark off each 10 mm round the circumference.
  d) Can you work out how to make this pattern?

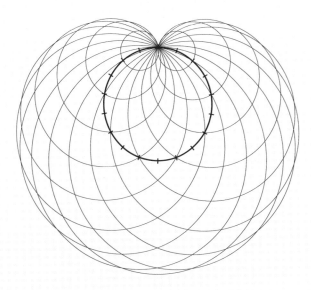

This pattern is called a cardioid.

The circumference

Remember: The circumference is the distance all the way round a circle.

Mathematicians have calculated that the circumference of a circle is about 3.14 or $3\frac{1}{7}$ ($\frac{22}{7}$) times the diameter. They call this number **pi** (after a letter in the Greek alphabet) and it is written: π.

The formula for calculating the circumference of a circle is:
circumference = π × diameter
$c = \pi d$

As the diameter is twice the radius, the formula for calculating the circumference of a circle is also:
circumference = 2π × radius
$c = 2\pi r$

Example 1
Calculate the circumference of a circle with a diameter of 18 cm.
$c - \pi d$
$\quad = 3.14 \times 18$
$\quad = 56.52 \, \text{cm}$

Example 2
Calculate the circumference of a circle with a radius of 6 cm.
$c = 2\pi r$
$\quad = 2 \times 3.14 \times 6$
$\quad = 37.68 \, \text{cm}$

1 Calculate the circumference of circles with the following diameters. Use $\pi = 3.14$.

a) 8 cm   b) 6 cm   c) 10 cm

d) 12.5 cm   e) 15 cm   f) 11.5 cm

g) 8.5 cm   h) 29 cm   i) 35 cm

2 Calculate the circumference of circles with the following radii. Use $\pi = 3.14$.

a) 8 cm   b) 6 cm   c) 14 cm

d) 18 cm   e) 10.5 cm   f) 11 cm

g) 17 cm   h) 8.5 cm   l) 12.5 cm

3 Measure the diameter of each circle to the nearest millimetre.
Calculate the circumference of each circle.

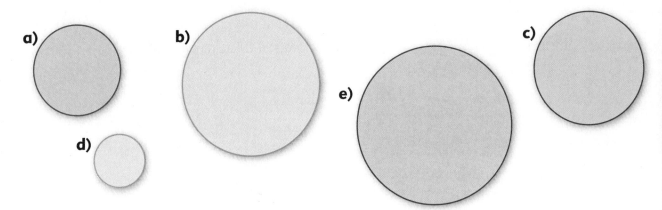

a)
b)
c)
d)
e)

4 A wheel has a radius of 50 cm.

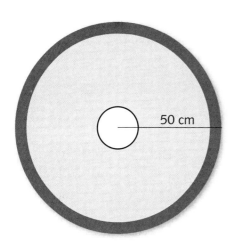

50 cm

a) How far will the wheel roll in 10 turns?

b) How far will it roll in 100 turns?

c) Approximately how many turns of the wheel will there be for it to travel 500 m?

Try this

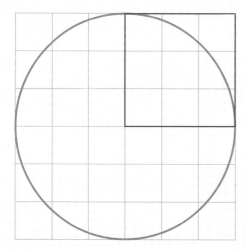

a) Count the squares to find the approximate area of this circle in cm².

b) A square has been drawn on the circle's radius. Write its area in cm².

c) Approximately how many times larger is the area of the circle than the area of the square?

Use centimetre-square paper and draw other circles. Draw a square on the circle's radius and answer these questions again.

What do you notice about all your answers to part (c)?

Constructing shapes

Compasses, a set-square, a protractor and a ruler are all tools useful for constructing shapes.

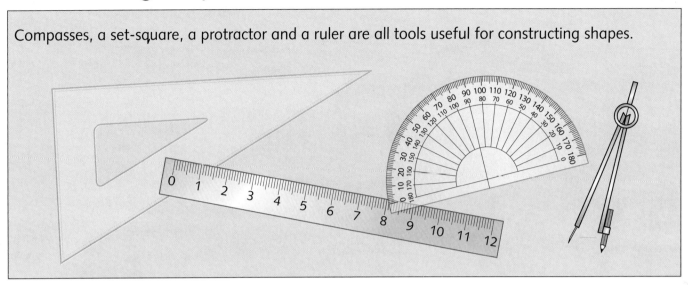

Construct these shapes.
Measure the length of x in each shape you have drawn.

❶

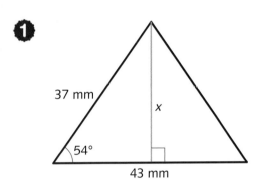

37 mm
x
54°
43 mm

❷

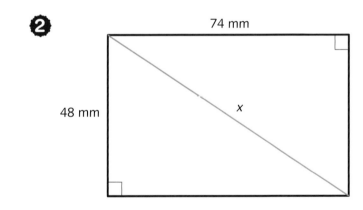

74 mm
48 mm
x

❸

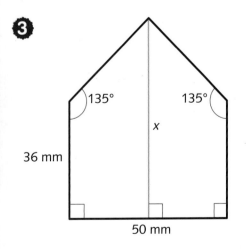

135°   135°
x
36 mm
50 mm

❹

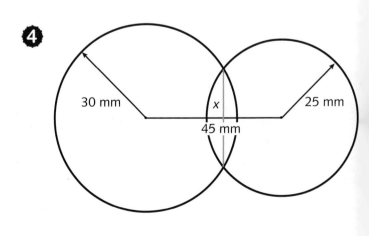

30 mm
x
25 mm
45 mm

5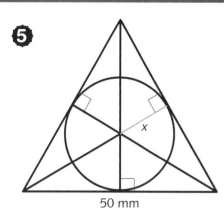

50 mm

6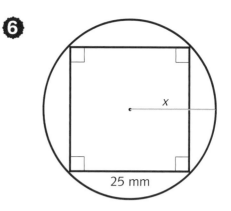

25 mm

Try this

An ellipse is a special oval with two lines of symmetry.
It is like a squashed circle.

This is a method for making an ellipse out of a circle.

a) Cut out a paper circle, radius 5 cm.
Mark a point A inside the circle.

b) Fold any part of the circumference to touch A.

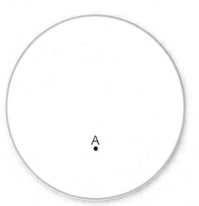

A

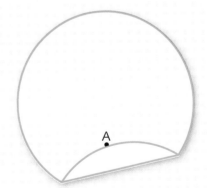

A

c) Make as many different folds of the circumference
to touch A as you can.
Your circle should then have an ellipse inside it.

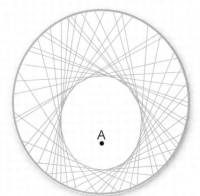

A

Rotational symmetry

A shape has **rotational symmetry** if it fits on top of itself more than once as it takes a complete turn.

The **order of rotational symmetry** is the number of times that the shape fits on top of itself.
This must be 2 or more. Shapes that only fit on themselves once have no rotational symmetry.

The **centre of rotation** (C) is the point about which the shape turns.

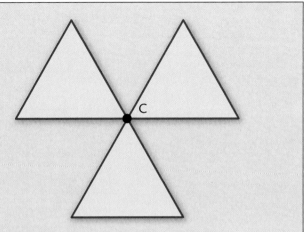

This shape has rotational symmetry of order 3 about its centre.

---

1 Trace each shape.
Use your tracing to check the rotational symmetry of each shape.
Write the order of rotational symmetry. Write 'none' if it has no rotational symmetry.

a)
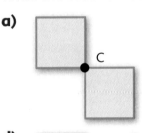

b)
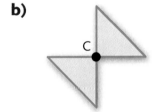

c)
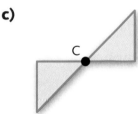

d)
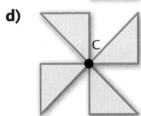

e)
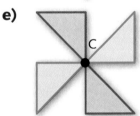

f)
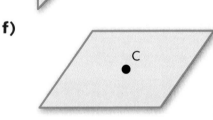

2 Copy each of these shapes on to squared paper.
Leave plenty of space between them.
Complete your shapes so that they have rotational symmetry of order 4 about C.

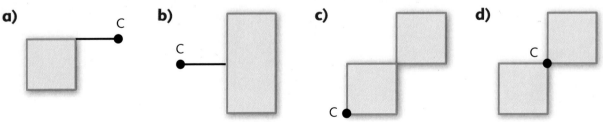

a)   b)   c)   d)

3 Shapes can be rotated clockwise or anti-clockwise. We use degrees of turn to show the rotation.

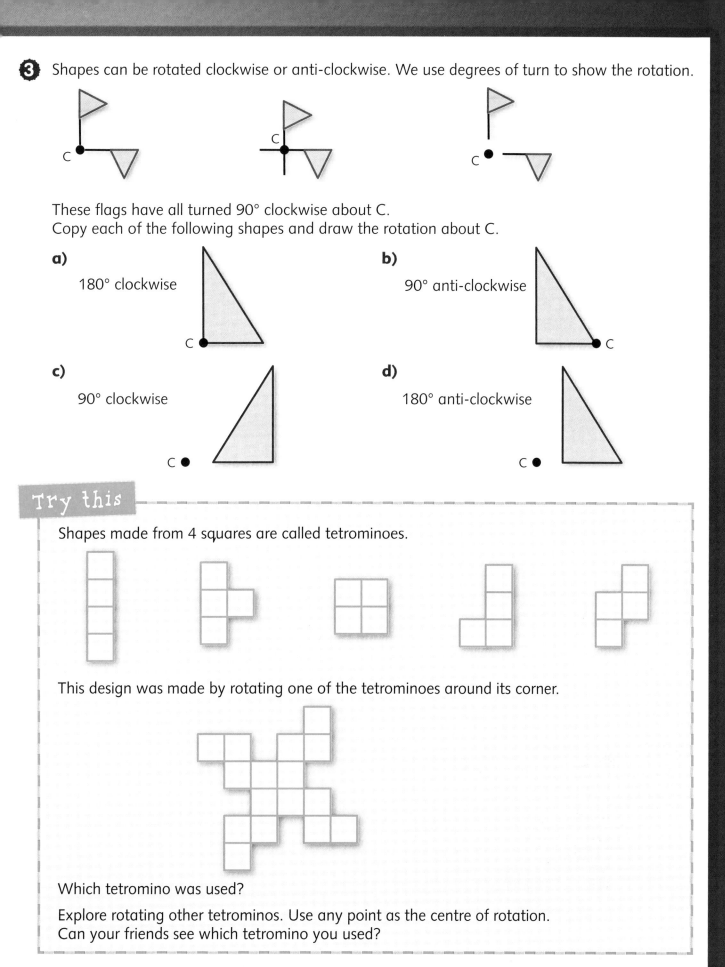

These flags have all turned 90° clockwise about C.
Copy each of the following shapes and draw the rotation about C.

a) 180° clockwise

b) 90° anti-clockwise

c) 90° clockwise

d) 180° anti-clockwise

Try this

Shapes made from 4 squares are called tetrominoes.

This design was made by rotating one of the tetrominoes around its corner.

Which tetromino was used?

Explore rotating other tetrominos. Use any point as the centre of rotation.
Can your friends see which tetromino you used?

Movement geometry

A shape can be moved by translation, reflection or rotation.

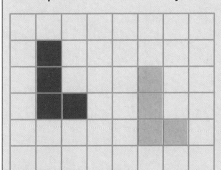

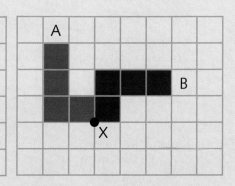

Translation: sliding a shape without rotating or flipping over. This shape has moved 4 squares across and 1 square down.

Reflection: this is sometimes called a 'flip'.

Rotation: a shape can be rotated about a point, clockwise or anti-clockwise.
Shape A is rotated clockwise around point X to become shape B.

1 Write whether these shapes have been **translated**, **rotated** or **reflected**.

a)

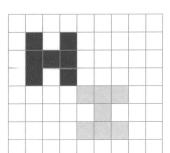

b)

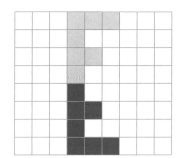

c)

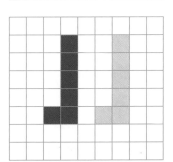

d)

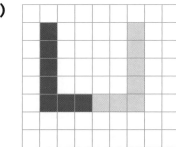

e)

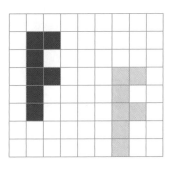

f)

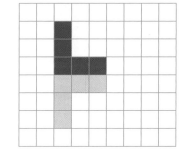

Construct these regular polygons.

1 Equilateral triangle

a) Draw a line AB 6 cm long.

b) Open your compasses to 6 cm.
Put the point on A and draw an arc.

c) Put your point on B and draw an arc to
cross the first one. Label this C.

d) Draw in AC and BC with a ruler.

2 Regular hexagon

a) Draw a circle of radius 3 cm.

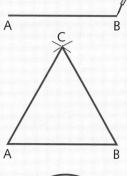

b) Keep your compasses open to 3 cm.
Go round the circumference of the circle
drawing arcs 3 cm apart.

c) Use a ruler to join the points where the
arcs cross the circle.

3 Answer these questions about the two shapes you have constructed.
   a) What is the length of each side of the two shapes?
   b) What are the angles of each shape?
   c) What is the order of rotational symmetry of each shape?

Lines and angles

1 What type of angle is this?

a) acute angle b) obtuse angle
c) reflex angle

2 What is the angle *x*?

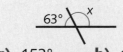

a) 153° b) 117° c) 50

3 Which line is parallel to AB?

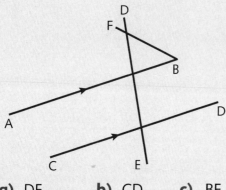

a) DE b) CD c) BF

4 What is angle *x*?

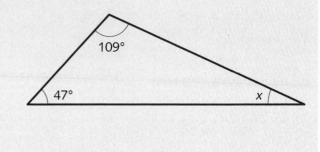

a) 24° b) 34° c) 44°

5 Copy and complete these drawings using a ruler and set-square.

a) Draw a line CE from point E, perpendicular to CD. Make the line CE = 46 mm.

b) Draw a line through point F, perpendicular to GH. Label the line JK, and make the line JK = 62 mm.

c) Draw a parallel line to AB going through point C

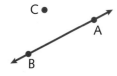

d) Draw a parallel line to XY going through point A.

6 Draw a rectangle of side length 38 mm and 56 mm. Use a set-square and ruler to draw parallel and perpendicular lines.

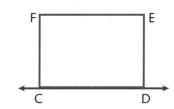

7 Calculate the size of the missing angles on each of these. Do not use a protractor.

a)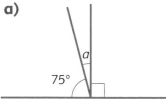

b)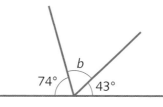

c)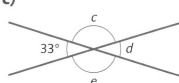

d)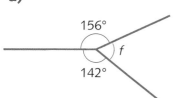

e)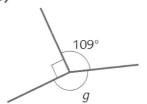

f)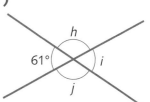

8 Calculate the size of the missing angles on each of these. Do not use a protractor.

a)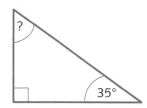

b)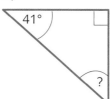

c)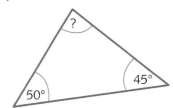

d)

e)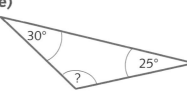

f)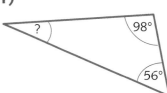

9 What are the missing angles on these quadrilaterals?

a) trapezium   **b)** rhombus   **c)** parallelogram   **d)** kite

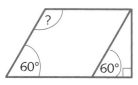

These are the wooden frames on a building site.
EF is parallel to XY.
What is angle *b*?

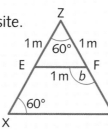

Polygons and polyhedra

1 Which of these quadrilaterals has 1 line of symmetry?

a)

b)

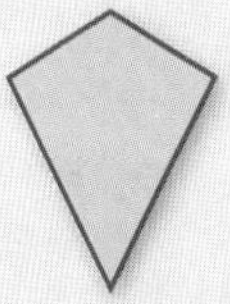

c)

2 Which of these is the net of a cuboid?

a)   b) 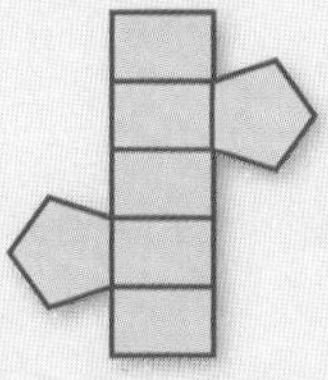   c)

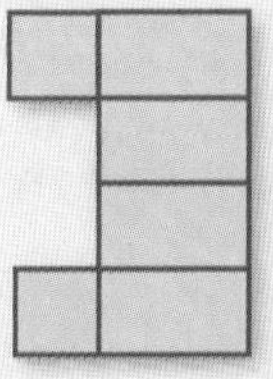

3 Which of these is a rhombus?

a)   b)

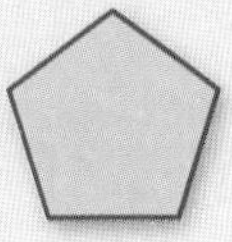

c)

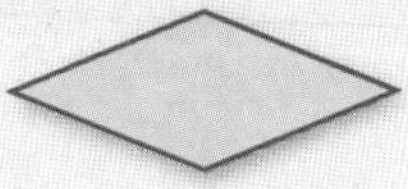

4 How many edges does a pentagonal prism have?

a) 10   b) 20   c) 15

5 Copy and complete these sentences by writing **always**, **sometimes** or **never**.

a) A triangle [ ] has 3 acute angles.

b) A triangle [ ] has 2 obtuse angles.

c) A triangle [ ] has 2 perpendicular sides.

d) A triangle [ ] has 2 parallel sides.

e) An isosceles triangle [ ] has an obtuse angle.

f) An equilateral triangle [ ] has 3 lines of symmetry.

6 Anna's dictionary gives this definition for a parallelogram:
A parallelogram is a quadrilateral that has two pairs of parallel edges.

Using this definition, say which of these is a parallelogram.

a)   b) 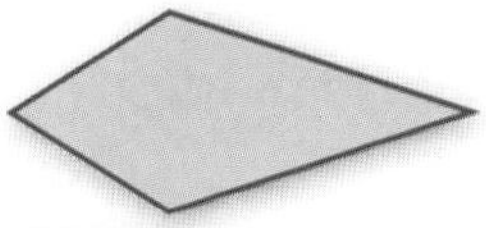   c)

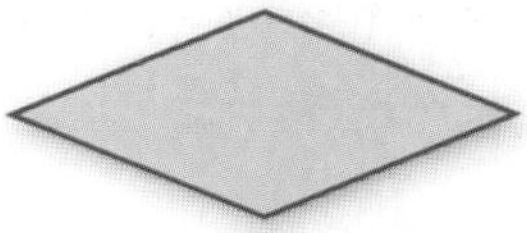

d)   e)   f)

7 Which shapes are congruent to these two triangles?
Which shapes are similar to the triangles?

a)

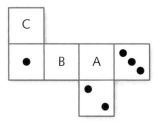

A   B   C   D   E   F

b)

A   B   C   D   E   F

8 Opposite faces of a dice add up to seven.
This is the net of a dice.
How many spots would go on faces A, B and C?

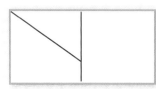

9 This a net of a cube with tabs for gluing.

When it is folded up, edge LK will stick to edge JK.
a) What edge will AB stick to?
b) Which two letters will meet at point E?
c) Make a copy of the net, so that each edge is 3 cm long.
Cut out your net and fold it up.
Use your net to check your answers for parts (a) and (b).

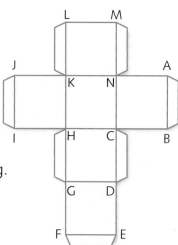

Try this

Two lines have been drawn in each rectangle to make new shapes.

1 triangle, 1 square and 1 trapezium   3 triangles and 1 pentagon

Make 6 copies of this rectangle.

Draw two lines in each rectangle to make these new shapes.

a) 3 triangles

b) 4 quadrilaterals

c) 2 triangles and 2 quadrilaterals

d) 4 isosceles triangles

e) 1 rectangle and 2 right-angled triangles

f) 2 trapeziums and 2 right-angled triangles

Geometry problems

1 How has this shape been moved?

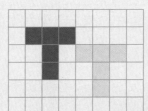

a) rotation
b) translation
c) reflection

2 If the radius of a circle is 8.2 cm, what is the diameter?

a) 4.1 cm   b) 11.34 cm   c) 16.4 cm

3 What is the name of this part of a circle?

a) radius
b) circumference
c) diameter

4 If the diameter of a circle is 19 cm, what is the radius?

a) 38 cm   b) 8 cm   c) 9.5 cm

5 Copy and label these parts of a circle.

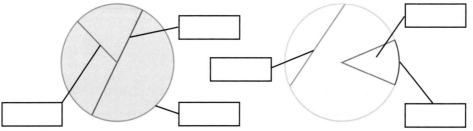

6 Look at these symbols.

A   B    C    D   E

a) How many lines of symmetry are there for each symbol?
b) What is the order of rotational symmetry for each symbol?

7 This triangle has been rotated 180° around point C. The triangle and its rotation make a parallelogram.

Copy each triangle.
Use tracing paper to give each triangle a 180° turn about C.
Write the name of each quadrilateral that you make.

a)   b)   c)   d)   e)

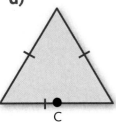
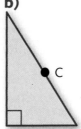
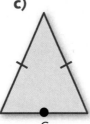
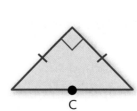
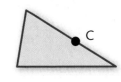

8 Construct these shapes accurately.
Measure and label the length of x in millimetres and the size of angle y in degrees.

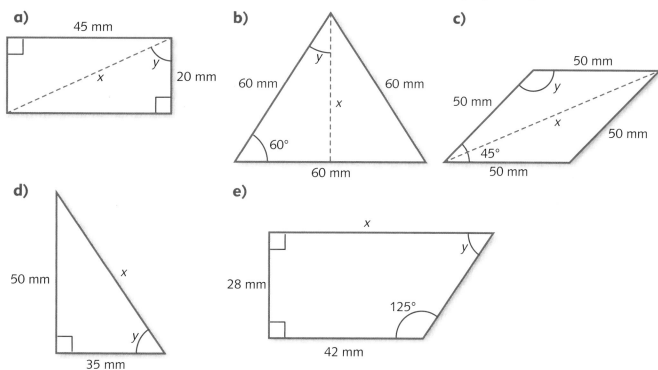

a)
45 mm
20 mm

b)
60 mm   60 mm
60°
60 mm

c)
50 mm
50 mm   50 mm
45°   50 mm   50 mm

d)
50 mm
35 mm

e)
28 mm
125°
42 mm

Try this

Investigate spiral patterns on squared paper.

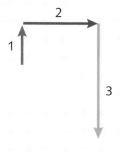

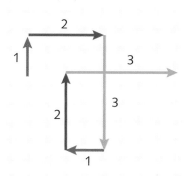

final shape

This is a 1, 2, 3 spiral, turning clockwise.

Keep repeating the lines:
1 square long then turn, 2 squares long then turn, 3 squares long then turn…

Always remember to turn in the same clockwise direction.

Try a 1, 2, 3 spiral then investigate others:

3, 1, 2   **2, 1, 1**   **4, 1, 3**

Look for patterns in your spiral shapes.

Macmillan Education
Between Towns Road, Oxford OX4 3PP
A division of Macmillan Publishers Limited
Companies and representatives throughout the world

ISBN 978-0-230-02834-0

First published in 2010

Designed by Andy Magee Design
Typeset by Tek-Art, Crawley Down, West Sussex
Illustrated by Tek-Art
Cover design by Bigtop Design Limited
The authors and publishers would like to thank the following
for permission to reproduce their photographic material:
Cover Photography: Clark Wiseman/www.studio-8.co.uk
Alamy/B.O'Kane p49
Photolibrary/Calvin Nicholls p7

Printed and bound in Egypt by Sahara Printing Company

2012 2011 2010
10 9 8 7 6 5 4 3 2 1